SADLIER-OXFORD

LEVEL H

Vocabulary Workshop

Enhanced Edition

The classic program for:

- *developing* and *enhancing* vocabulary resources

- *promoting* more effective communication in today's world

- *improving* vocabulary skills assessed on standardized and/or college-admission tests

By
Jerome Shostak

Sadlier-Oxford

A Division of William H. Sadlier, Inc.
9 Pine Street
New York, NY 10005-1002
1-800-221-5175

Contents

Copyright © 1996 by
Sadlier-Oxford,
A Division of
William H. Sadlier, Inc.

ISBN: 0-8215-0613-7
123456789/98765

Home Office: 9 Pine Street
New York, NY 10005-1002
1-800-221-5175

Foreword

For close to five decades VOCABULARY WORKSHOP has been a highly successful tool for guiding and stimulating systematic vocabulary growth for students. It has also been extremely valuable for preparing students to take the types of standardized vocabulary tests commonly used to assess grade placement, competence for graduation, and/or college readiness. The *Enhanced Edition* has faithfully maintained those features that have made the program so beneficial in these two areas, while introducing new elements to keep abreast of changing times and changing standardized-test procedures, particularly the SAT. The features that make VOCABULARY WORKSHOP so valuable include:

Word List

Each book contains 300 or more basic words, selected on the basis of:
- currency in present-day usage
- frequency on recognized vocabulary lists
- applicability to standardized tests
- current grade-placement research

Units

The words in each book are organized around 15 short, stimulating *Units* featuring:
- pronunciation and parts of speech

New!
- definitions—fuller treatment in *Enhanced Edition*
- synonyms and antonyms
- usage—one phrase and two sentences illustrating literal and abstract/figurative uses of each basic word

Reviews

Five *Reviews* highlight and reinforce the work of the units through challenging exercises involving:

New!
- shades of meaning (SAT-type critical-thinking exercise)
- definitions
- synonyms and antonyms
- analogies
- sentence completions
- word families
- more

Cumulative Reviews

Four *Cumulative Reviews* utilize standardized testing techniques to provide ongoing assessment of word mastery, all involving SAT-type critical-thinking skills. Here the exercises revolve around

New!
- shades of meaning
- analogies
- two-word completions

Additional Features

- A *Diagnostic Test* provides ready assessment of student needs at the outset of the term.
- The *Vocabulary of Vocabulary* reviews terms and concepts needed for effective word study.
- The *Final Mastery Test* provides end-of-term assessment of student achievement.
- *Building with Word Roots* introduces the study of etymology.
- *Enhancing Your Vocabulary,* Levels F through H, introduces students to the study of word clusters.

New!
- *Working with Parts of Speech,* Levels F through H, provides further work with word clusters and introduces 45 new words per level.

Ancillary Materials

- An *Answer Key* for each level supplies answers to all materials in the student text.
- A *Series Teacher's Guide* provides a thorough overview of the features in each level, along with practical tips for using them.
- The *Supplementary Testing Program: Cycle One, Cycle Two* provides two complete programs of separate and different testing materials for each level so testing can be varied. A *Combined Answer Key* for each level is also available.
- The SAT-type *TEST PREP Blackline Masters* for each level provide further testing materials designed to help students prepare for SAT-type standardized tests. (Answers are included in each booklet.)
- The *Interactive Audio Pronunciation Program* is also available for each level.

Pronunciation Key

The pronunciation is indicated for every basic word introduced in this book. The symbols used for this purpose, as listed below, are similar to those appearing in most standard dictionaries of recent vintage. The author has consulted a large number of dictionaries for this purpose but has relied primarily on *Webster's Third New International Dictionary* and *The Random House Dictionary of the English Language (Unabridged)*.

There are, of course, many English words for which two (or more) pronunciations are commonly accepted. In virtually all cases where such words occur in this book, the author has sought to make things easier for the student by giving just one pronunciation. The only significant exception occurs when the pronunciation changes in accordance with a shift in the part of speech. Thus we would indicate that *project* in the verb form is pronounced prə 'jekt, and in the noun form, 'proj ekt.

It is believed that these relatively simple pronunciation guides will be readily usable by the student. It should be emphasized, however, that the *best* way to learn the pronunciation of a word is to listen to and imitate an educated speaker.

Vowels					
ā	lake	e	stress	oi	*oi*l
a	mat	ī	kn*i*fe	û	*u*rn
â	care	i	s*i*t	ü	l*oo*t, new
ä	b*a*rk, b*o*ttle	o	box	u̇	f*oo*t, p*u*ll
au̇	d*ou*bt	ō	flow	ə	r*u*g, brok*e*n
ē	beat, word*y*	ô	*a*ll, c*o*rd	ər	b*i*rd, bett*er*

Consonants					
ch	*ch*ild, lecture	s	*c*ellar	wh	*wh*at
g	*g*ive	sh	*sh*un	y	*y*earn
j	*g*entle, bri*dg*e	th	*th*ank	z	i*s*
ŋ	si*ng*	t͟h	*th*ose	zh	mea*s*ure

All other consonants are sounded as in the alphabet.

Stress   The accent mark *precedes* the syllable receiving the major stress: en 'rich

Parts of Speech					
adj.	adjective	*int.*	interjection	*prep.*	preposition
adv.	adverb	*n.*	noun	*v.*	verb
		part.	participle		
		pl.	plural		

The Vocabulary of Vocabulary

English is rich in vocabulary that is particularly useful for describing and discussing the use and abuse of words. By mastering technical and quasi-technical terms of this kind, you will equip yourself to deal more clearly and forcefully with many linguistic problems.

Below are some terms that you should know. The exercises that follow will give you a chance to practice and gain full mastery of these specialized words.

I. *From the list of words below, choose the one that **best completes** each of the following sentences. Write it in the appropriate space.*

alliteration	euphemism	malapropism	neologism
counterword	generics	metonymy	prolixity
epigram	litotes	mixed metaphor	sesquipedalian

1. A brief, witty saying is called a(n) _____ .

2. _____ is the repetition of an initial consonant in a series of words. It is also known as *head rhyme* or *initial rhyme*.

3. Longwindedness is often called _____ .

4. A(n) _____ is a substitution of a mild or inoffensive expression for one that may shock or offend.

5. Brand names that have become general terms in the language are often called

_____ .

6. _____ is a term that means *characterized by the use of long words* or *having many syllables* and often leads to gobbledygook.

7. A(n) _____ is a word that is commonly used so vaguely that it ceases to convey any real meaning in a given context.

8. The combination of two or more inconsistent comparisons always results in a(n)

_____ .

9. The unintentionally humorous substitution of a similar-sounding word or phrase for

the expression intended is termed a(n) _____ .

10. A newly coined word is a(n) _____ .

11. _____ is the figure of speech in which an idea is expressed by using a term designating or exemplifying some associated notion.

12. _____ is a figure of speech in which the affirmative is expressed by negating or denying the opposite.

II. *From the terms listed above, choose the one that is **most appropriate** for each of the following, and write it in the space provided.*

1. a not entirely uneventful life   _____

2. Answering the question "How was the trip?" by listing the menu of every meal eaten for the six days on the road   _____

3. nice, awful, great, cool, yummy _____

4. demanded that City Hall take action _____

5. Your clear conscience is the result of a poor memory. _____

6. Formica; aspirin; Ping-Pong _____

7. cyberspace, skyjack, simulcast _____

8. Our country is a tower of strength that shows every sign of forging ahead to new heights of power. _____

9. antidisestablishmentarianism _____

10. "Fifty-four forty or fight!" _____

11. "a strategic withdrawal" instead of "a retreat" _____

12. "It's not the heat, it's the humility." _____

III. _Explain in your own words what, if anything, **is wrong** in each of the following statements._

1. All their neat plans for improving the gym or whatever fell through at the last moment.

2. Capital punishment is a known detergent of crime.

3. You know, it was cool of you to do your thing for us at the concert.

4. "The only thing we have to fear is fear itself!"

5. It was just a pigment of my imagination.

6. The librarian accused him of bibliophilistic pilferage.

7. Put a tiger in your tank, and your car will get along swimmingly.

8. If anything goes wrong during the flight, you can always use your aerodynamic personnel decelerator.

9. With a terrific quarterback, dynamite receivers, and a stiffer defense, our team is sure to have a fabulous season.

10. "I spend most of my day at my tripewriter, preparing official administrivia," the secretary remarked.

11. Maybe if we listened, history would stop repeating itself.

12. The Philadelphia Eagles are considered the underdogs in this evening's game.

13. Fjords are Swedish automobiles.

14. Surveillance should precede saltation.

15. Like dead, remembered footsteps on the floor, the road was a ribbon of moonlight.

16. During the early days of the Depression, the slowdown accelerated week by week.

17. A moiety of a farinaceous, rectangularly molded mass subjected to adequate heat is preferable to nullity.

Diagnostic Test

The following test contains a sampling of the words that are found in the units of this Vocabulary Workshop. It will give you an idea of the nature of the words to be studied. When you have completed all the units, the Final Mastery Test will measure what you have learned. By comparing your results on the Final Mastery Test with your results on the Diagnostic Test, you will be able to judge your progress.

Synonyms Circle the letter of the word or expression that is most nearly the **synonym** of the word in **boldface type** in the introductory phrase.

1. a **risible** development
a. unexpected   b. fortunate   c. laughable   d. recent

2. **opt** to leave
a. prepare   b. refuse   c. choose   d. fail

3. **gambol** on the green
a. romp   b. lie   c. sleep   d. loiter

4. find the **mot juste**
a. perfect gift   b. right word   c. lost child   d. trouble spot

5. **adjudicate** the dispute
a. define   b. mediate   c. overhear   d. start

6. my **bête noire**
a. nemesis   b. success   c. favorite   d. aspiration

7. an **insouciant** attitude
a. serious   b. ambivalent   c. carefree   d. phlegmatic

8. a **maudlin** story
a. hilarious   b. terrifying   c. long   d. sentimental

9. a terrible **faux pas**
a. job   b. pain   c. loss   d. blunder

10. an **ecumenical** conference
a. financial   b. worldwide   c. moral   d. uninteresting

11. **condescend** to see us
a. refuse   b. stoop   c. attempt   d. plan

12. **chimerical** hopes
a. buoyant   b. unrealistic   c. modest   d. achievable

13. a **niggardly** allowance
a. generous   b. lavish   c. adequate   d. stingy

14. **sub-rosa** campaign contributions
a. covert   b. legal   c. exceptional   d. routine

15. receive something as a **lagniappe**
a. bonus   b. warning   c. visitor   d. honor

16. a **noisome** atmosphere
a. charming   b. noxious   c. loud   d. explosive

17. the **bane** of my life
a. mainstay   b. joy   c. hobby   d. ruin

18. begin **in medias res**
a. again   b. at the beginning   c. in the middle   d. at the conclusion

19. a **quizzical** look
a. solemn   b. caustic   c. querulous   d. puzzled

20. a **touchstone** of valor
a. medal   b. yardstick   c. champion   d. amulet

Antonyms   *Circle the letter of the word that is most nearly the **opposite** in meaning to the item in **boldface type** in the introductory phrase.*

21. a **diaphanous** curtain
a. opaque   b. flimsy   c. colorful   d. full

22. an inexplicable sense of **euphoria**
a. happiness   b. drowsiness   c. contentment   d. melancholy

23. a **gargantuan** appetite
a. depraved   b. tiny   c. stimulated   d. immense

24. deliver a lengthy **philippic**
a. panegyric   b. diatribe   c. harangue   d. invective

25. a **lackluster** performance
a. early   b. dazzling   c. exhausting   d. mediocre

26. **quixotic** schemes
a. fanciful   b. extravagant   c. realistic   d. visionary

27. a **waggish** fellow
a. mature   b. childish   c. unbalanced   d. dour

28. **apropos of** our discussion
a. irrelevant to   b. needed for   c. germane to   d. stemming from

29. **constrict** the flow
a. control   b. end   c. inspect   d. enlarge

30. an **ineluctable** conclusion
a. tragic   b. decisive   c. avoidable   d. peaceful

31. a **viable** arrangement
a. attractive   b. impracticable   c. reasonable   d. dangerous

32. **minuscule** amounts
a. small   b. huge   c. unknown   d. profitable

33. an **apocryphal** story
a. authentic   b. fictitious   c. romantic   d. sordid

34. a **mellifluous** voice
a. sweet   b. unusual   c. low   d. shrill

35. a **malleable** mind
a. costly   b. indestructible   c. intractable   d. brilliant

Unit 1

Group A

adjunct	fait accompli
bellwether	hidebound
caterwaul	hierarchy
chimerical	liturgy
effete	mirage

Pronunciation Match each of the words contained in Group A with its phonetic transcription. Write the appropriate word in the blank space provided at the right.

1. ′lit ər jē _____

2. fe ta kôm ′plē _____

3. ′kat ər wôl _____

4. ′aj ənkt _____

5. ′hīd baủnd _____

6. mi ′räzh _____

7. ′bel weth ər _____

8. i ′fēt _____

9. kī ′mer i kəl _____

10. ′hī ə rär kē _____

Definition Choose the word from Group A that most nearly corresponds to each of the definitions below. Write the word in the blank space at the right of the definition and then in the illustrative phrase below it.

1. (v.) to howl or screech like a cat; to quarrel; (n.) a harsh or noisy cry; a racket _____

kept awake by their _____

2. (n.) an accomplished and presumably irreversible deed, fact, or action _____

present them with a(n) _____

3. (n.) something illusory, without substance, or without a basis in reality; an illusion _____

deceived by a(n) _____ in the desert

4. (n.) something added to something else as helpful or useful but not essential; an assistant or helper; a valuable quality or characteristic; (adj.) added or connected in a subordinate capacity; attached to a faculty or staff in an auxiliary capacity _____

a(n) _____ professor

5. (*n.*) any system of things or people arranged or graded one above another in order of rank, wealth, class, etc.

the governmental _____

6. (*n.*) the male sheep that leads the flock to the slaughterhouse; a leader, as in a desperate or violent undertaking; an indicator of trends

the _____ in the uprising

7. (*n.*) a religious service or rite; the form of a ritual or other act of public worship

revise the _____

8. (*adj.*) narrow-minded and rigid, especially in opinions or prejudices; stubbornly and unthinkingly conservative

a(n) _____ pedant

9. (*adj.*) lacking in wholesome vigor or energy; worn-out or exhausted; sterile or unable to produce; out-of-date _____

a(n) _____ society

10. (*adj.*) absurd; wildly fantastic; impossible _____

a(n) _____ "get-rich-quick" scheme

Group B

morass　　　　　　　　**quasi-**
noisome　　　　　　　 **raillery**
oblivious　　　　　　　**ribald**
poltroon　　　　　　　 **supine**
proselyte　　　　　　　**vignette**

Pronunciation　　Match each of the words contained in Group B with its phonetic transcription. Write the appropriate word in the blank space provided at the right.

1. sù 'pīn _____

2. 'noi səm _____

3. ə 'bliv ē əs _____

4. vin 'yet _____

5. pol 'trün _____

6. 'rib əld _____

7. mə 'ras _____

8. 'pros ə līt   _____

9. 'kwā zī *or* 'kwä zē   _____

10. 'rā lər ē   _____

| **Definition** | *Choose the word from Group B that most nearly corresponds to each of the definitions below. Write the word in the blank space at the right of the definition and then in the illustrative phrase below it.* |

1. (*adj.*) lying flat on one's back; listless or lethargic; apathetic or passive   _____

    resting in a(n) _____ position

2. (*n.*) a patch of low, soft, wet ground; a swamp; a confusing situation in which one is entrapped, as in quicksand   _____

    wallowing in a _____ of self-doubt

3. (*n.*) a short description or sketch; a picture or illustration with edges that gradually shade off; a decorative design on the title page of a book or at the beginning or end of a chapter   _____

    _____ of country life

4. (*n.*) a convert; a disciple   _____

    a group of zealous _____

5. (*adj.*) offensive or disgusting; foul-smelling; harmful or injurious   _____

    the _____ atmosphere of a slaughterhouse

6. (*adj.*) irreverently mocking; coarse, vulgar, or indecent in language   _____

    fond of telling _____ stories

7. (*adj.*) forgetful; unaware   _____

    completely _____ of the dangers involved

8. (*n.*) good-humored ridicule; teasing   _____

    the good-natured _____ of the locker room

9. (*n.*) a base coward   _____

    caught the _____ in the act of deserting

10. (*adj.*) resembling but not actually being; seemingly but not actually or completely; (*adv.*) partly, somewhat, or to some degree (*used in combination*)   _____

    a(n) _____ military organization

Completing the Sentence *Choose the word for this unit that best completes each of the following sentences. Write it in the space given.*

1. Cynics may say that the goal of universal and lasting peace is no more than a(n) _____ , but we must continue to hope and strive for it as though it were an attainable possibility.

2. The newspaper published a series of charming _____ by my Aunt Alice—brief sketches of the town she grew up in and of the way of life of an earlier, more placid day.

3. The local Parents' Association has on many occasions served as a willing _____ to the administration and staff of our school, and I am sure that we can depend upon its support in the present crisis.

4. I think that the critic was a little harsh when he observed that the band's lead vocalist did not sing so much as _____ .

5. With the unlimited faith and boundless courage of a die-hard fanatic, Don Quixote dismissed as a mere _____ anyone who refused to join in his crusade against the forces of evil.

6. Ever since she learned of the failure of her project, she has been mired in a(n) _____ of disappointment and self-recrimination.

7. A handful of self-appointed "leaders" served as the _____ who induced the mob to surge through the barriers.

8. As a rule, I am not a particularly proud or combative person, but I cannot be _____ to the fact that you have deliberately insulted me.

9. As late as the 17th century, researchers called "alchemists" devoted their lives to the pursuit of _____ schemes for turning iron and other base metals into gold.

10. Their youthful enthusiasm for literature had degenerated over the years into a(n) _____ preoccupation with quibbling criticism and minor details of scholarship.

11. If you think that the literature of earlier ages was always staid and proper, take a look at some of the _____ stories in the *Decameron,* written more than 600 years ago.

12. Polluted by the spill from a nearby chemical plant, the once beautiful lake had become a foul pool, _____ and hideous.

13. I regret Fred's resignation as much as anyone, but I think that we must regard it as a(n) _____ and find someone to take his place.

14. Failure in itself is no disgrace, but the _____ acceptance of failure certainly is.

15. The advocates of equal rights maintain that we must rid ourselves of the

_____ prejudices that bar the physically impaired from many
occupations.

16. Since the Smithsonian Institution is only partly under the control of the

United States government, it is considered a(n) _____
governmental institution.

17. She used talent, charm, energy, and determination to fight her way up the

corporate _____ until she attained the highest position in
the company.

18. Taking advantage of the young man's naive idealism, they sought to make

him a(n) _____ to serve in their wild revolutionary plots.

19. The use of English rather than traditional languages in religious ceremonies

is evidence of efforts to modernize and revitalize the _____
of various denominations.

20. I detected an undertone of hostility and ridicule in the remarks, which were

ostensibly no more than good-natured _____ .

Synonyms   *Choose the word for this unit that is most nearly the* ***same*** *in meaning as each of the following items. Write it in the space given.*

1. a convert, novice, disciple, neophyte   _____

2. a thumbnail sketch, anecdote   _____

3. prone, prostrate; inert, apathetic   _____

4. fanciful, visionary, quixotic, pie-in-the-sky   _____

5. a swamp, bog, quagmire   _____

6. forgetful; unaware, insensible   _____

7. banter, teasing, persiflage; ridicule   _____

8. an optical illusion, will-o'-the-wisp   _____

9. narrow-minded, intolerant, inflexible   _____

10. decadent, sterile, enfeebled; outmoded   _____

11. to howl, whine; a wail, screech   _____

12. bawdy, indecent; risqué; coarse, vulgar   _____

13. resembling, kind of, semi-, as if   _____

14. a coward, craven, dastard, "chicken"   _____

15. an accomplished fact, irreversible situation _____

16. fetid, noxious; vile, loathsome _____

17. a ceremony, rite, ritual, observance _____

18. a chain of command, pecking order _____

19. an auxiliary, associate; an addition, accessory _____

20. a ringleader, initiator; a barometer _____

Antonyms   *Choose the word for this unit that is most nearly **opposite** in meaning to each of the following items. Write it in the blank given.*

1. open-minded, tolerant, liberal, progressive _____

2. realistic, down-to-earth, practicable _____

3. wholesome, pleasant, sweet-smelling _____

4. aware, mindful, cognizant, alert _____

5. thriving, burgeoning; vigorous, dynamic _____

6. upright, erect, perpendicular, vertical _____

7. a master, teacher, guide, guru _____

8. a hero, stalwart, gallant _____

9. seemly, decorous, proper, not smutty _____

10. a follower, imitator, emulator _____

11. totally, completely; actually, in fact _____

12. solid ground, bedrock, terra firma _____

13. an epic, full-length treatment _____

Choosing the Right Word   *Circle the **boldface** word that more satisfactorily completes each of the following sentences.*

1. I am willing to listen to any reasonable grievances you may have, but this constant (**caterwauling, hierarchy**) about trivia has exhausted my patience.

2. Almost incredibly, a formidable resistance movement had been organized by people whom we had always associated with (**supine, chimerical**) submission to authority.

3. By late imperial times, centuries of soft living had turned the once hardy Roman people into an (**oblivious, effete**) and indolent race.

1

4. Failure to stand up for your rights is not being "prudent" or "moderate"; it is the behavior of a (**poltroon, bellwether**).

5. Your serene confidence that "everything will come out all right in the end" may be reassuring, but it is no more than a (**morass, mirage**).

6. Financial analysts carefully watch the performance of certain stocks, which they regard as (**bellwethers, mirages**), for indications of economic trends.

7. The lyrics of the song, presented as though they were devastating wit, were in my opinion no more than a coarse and (**supine, ribald**) jest.

8. How can you expect a prompt response from an agency that is bogged down in a veritable (**morass, liturgy**) of unnecessary red tape?

9. With penetrating insight and a marvelous ear for dialogue, the author gave us in a few words an unforgettable (**adjunct, vignette**) of a confused but hopeful adolescent.

10. After a brief period of popularity, their cheap and vulgar novels lost their appeal and sank into well-deserved (**proselyte, oblivion**).

11. Her unfailing courtesy to others is not a mere (**adjunct, morass**) of her personality; it reflects the essential values and standards by which she lives.

12. A superintendent is at the head of the (**hierarchy, vignette**) of educators responsible for the schooling of our children and young people.

13. Overly sensitive to any suggestion of ridicule, young Rogers seemed to be hurt even by a friend's good-natured (**raillery, proselytes**).

14. They have confronted us not with a theoretical possibility but with a(n) (**adjunct, fait accompli**); now we must decide what we can do about it.

15. We have lived to see the acceptance and enactment of reform programs, that, when first proposed, were dismissed as absolutely (**chimerical, oblivious**).

16. He is so (**ribald, hidebound**) in his political views that he won't even listen to opinions that differ from his own.

17. As I listened to the talk of those unlettered folk, suffused with love and reverence, I felt that their simple words were a (**raillery, liturgy**) worthy of the respect of the most learned ecclesiastic.

18. Although the old Senator no longer holds any public office, her fame and prestige are so great that she is still regarded as a (**quasi-, hidebound**) public figure.

19. Martin Luther King appealed to his countrymen to abandon the (**noisome, quasi-**) stereotypes of racism and rise to a new level of understanding between the races.

20. The great historian Edward Gibbon sought to explain how and why the (**proselytizing, liturgical**) efforts of the early Christian church met with such extraordinary success.

Unit 2

Group A

aegis	eleemosynary
apprise	indigenous
bibulous	lachrymose
claque	lexicon
deracinate	melee

Pronunciation Match each of the words contained in Group A with its phonetic transcription. Write the appropriate word in the space given.

1. 'lak rə mōs _____

2. 'bib yə ləs _____

3. 'lek sə kən _____

4. 'mā lā _____

5. 'ē jis _____

6. el i 'mos ə ner ē _____

7. ə 'prīz _____

8. in 'dij ə nəs _____

9. di 'ras ə nāt _____

10. klak _____

Definition Choose the word from Group A that most nearly corresponds to each of the definitions below. Write the word in the blank space at the right of the definition and then in the illustrative phrase below it.

1. (*adj.*) given to tears or weeping; causing to shed tears; mournful, lugubrious _____

a(n) _____ tale of poverty and woe

2. (*adj.*) fond of or inclined to drink; absorbent _____

a(n) _____ old codger

3. (*n.*) protection; patronage; sponsorship _____

under the _____ of UNESCO

4. (*n.*) a confused struggle; a violent free-for-all; a tumultuous mingling _____

mauled in the _____

5. (*n.*) a group of people hired to applaud a performer or performance; enthusiastic or fawning admirers; an opera hat _____

the soprano's _____

2

6. (*adj.*) originating in the country or region where found, native; inborn; inherent _____

wildlife _____ to the Canadian Rockies

7. (*v.*) to pull up by the roots; to root out, uproot, or dislocate; to eliminate all traces of _____

strive to _____ prejudice from our society

8. (*adj.*) charitable; dependent upon or supported by charity; derived from or provided by charity _____

_____ institutions ·

9. (*v.*) to inform of; to make aware of by giving oral or written notice _____

will _____ us of the latest developments

10. (*n.*) a dictionary of a language; the special vocabulary of a person, group, or subject; a compendium _____

the growing _____ of computer terminology

Group B

microcosm
minuscule
obfuscate
paternalism
polarize

purview
sanguine
solecism
vassal
verisimilitude

Pronunciation   *Match each of the words contained in Group B with its phonetic transcription. Write the appropriate word in the space given.*

1. 'pər vyü _____

2. 'sol ə siz əm _____

3. 'po lə rīz _____

4. ver ə si 'mil ə tüd _____

5. 'mī krə kos əm _____

6. 'vas əl _____

7. 'min əs kyül _____

8. pə 'tûr nə liz əm _____

9. 'saŋ gwin _____

10. 'ob fə skāt _____

Definition   Choose the word from Group B that most nearly corresponds to each of the definitions below. Write the word in the blank space at the right of the definition and then in the illustrative phrase below it.

1. (*n.*) a person under the protection of a feudal lord to whom he or she owes allegiance; a subordinate or dependent; a servant; (*adj.*) subservient _____

    the duke's _____

2. (*v.*) to cause to concentrate around two conflicting or contrasting positions; to cause light to vibrate in a pattern _____

    _____ public opinion on the issue

3. (*v.*) to darken or obscure; to confuse or bewilder _____

    _____ the meaning

4. (*n.*) the quality of appearing to be true, real, likely, or probable _____

    praised the novel's _____

5. (*adj.*) very small, tiny; (*n.*) a lowercase letter _____

    a(n) _____ portion

6. (*n.*) a miniature world or universe; a group or system viewed as the model of a larger group or system _____

    saw the ship as a(n) _____ of society

7. (*n.*) the policy or practice of treating or governing people in the manner of a father dealing with his children _____

    an attitude of benevolent _____

8. (*adj.*) having a ruddy complexion; of a naturally cheerful, confident, or optimistic outlook _____

    _____ about our chances of success

9. (*n.*) the range, extent, or scope of something; in law, the scope or limit of what is provided in a statute _____

    outside the _____ of my authority

10. (*n.*) a substandard or ungrammatical usage; a breach of etiquette; any impropriety or mistake _____

    a common _____ , such as "irregardless"

Completing the Sentence   Choose the word for this unit that best completes each of the following sentences. Write it in the space given.

1. Only within recent years has a complete _____ of the Latin language been compiled.

2. The third period was marred by a bench-clearing _____ that left the hockey rink littered with discarded gloves and sticks.

3. He is described by his associates as a(n) "_____ elderly gentleman," but if he were less wealthy and less socially prominent, he would probably be called just an old drunk.

4. No matter how fantastic and far-fetched the themes of Ray Bradbury's stories may be, he seems able to achieve an extraordinary effect of

_____ .

5. Surprisingly, the white potato, which I have always associated with Ireland, is _____ to the Americas.

6. When South Korea was invaded, the United States organized a collective defense effort under the _____ of the United Nations.

7. Both sides let on that the negotiators were still miles apart, when in fact the distance that separated them was _____ .

8. At the outset of World War II, Lithuania lost its sovereignty and became an unwilling _____ of the Soviet Union.

9. The issue is basically a simple one, and your efforts to _____ it by raising endless technical objections will have no effect on us.

10. He came to realize that the crowded inner city in which he had been born and raised was like a(n) _____ of the conflicts, sufferings, and needs of poor people all over the world.

11. I am not given to undue optimism, but the preliminary results of the polls make me _____ about the outcome of the election.

12. The European immigrants to America had a very difficult adjustment to make because they were _____ , psychologically as well as physically, from their Old World environment.

13. Without expressing opinions, simply _____ us as promptly as possible of the results of the conference.

14. A hard-line speech of that kind may indeed gain her the applause of her followers, but its overall effect will be to _____ sentiments throughout the country and impair national unity.

15. The people of this impoverished area need a program that will "help them to help themselves" — not a form of _____ that will make them completely dependent on outside aid.

16. A case of that type, which does not involve a Federal law or constitutional issue, does not come within the _____ of the Supreme Court.

17. It is easy for a person to be cynical about the motives that lie behind their

_____ activities, but I choose to believe that they sincerely want to help people.

18. Is the expression "It is me" to be regarded as a(n) _____ or as an acceptable idiomatic form?

19. If you are ever to get out of this tangled mess, now is the time for action,

not indulgence in _____ self-pity.

20. She defended her policy of hiring a(n) _____ by observing that even when an audience truly likes a performer, someone is needed to get the applause started.

Synonyms   *Choose the word for this unit that is most nearly the **same** in meaning as each of the following groups of expressions. Write it in the space given.*

1. realism, lifelikeness, authenticity   _____

2. patronage, sponsorship, auspices   _____

3. a fracas, brawl, scuffle, donnybrook   _____

4. scope, range, jurisdiction, orbit   _____

5. to acquaint, notify, inform   _____

6. charitable, philanthropic, beneficent   _____

7. a fan club; flatterers, hangers-on   _____

8. a wordbook, dictionary, glossary   _____

9. tearful, mournful, doleful, dolorous   _____

10. a dependent, menial, minion, servant   _____

11. ruddy, flushed; optimistic, rosy   _____

12. to split, divide, alienate, estrange   _____

13. to obscure, confuse, muddy the waters   _____

14. native, endemic, domestic, homegrown   _____

15. to extirpate, eradicate, expunge   _____

16. a mistake, misusage, blunder, faux pas   _____

17. infinitesimal, tiny, insignificant   _____

18. fond of the bottle, inebrious, alcoholic   _____

19. benevolence, solicitude, fatherliness   _____

20. an epitome, model; the world in little   _____

2

Antonyms   *Choose the word for this unit that is most nearly **opposite** in meaning to each of the following groups of expressions. Write it in the space given.*

1. to clarify, elucidate, explicate   _____

2. bloodless, ashen; pessimistic, gloomy   _____

3. to unite, unify, reconcile   _____

4. foreign, alien, exoteric, imported   _____

5. to implant, nurture, foster, instill   _____

6. an overlord   _____

7. teetotaling, abstemious, temperate   _____

8. dry-eyed; cheerful, merry, hilarious   _____

9. selfish, self-seeking, uncharitable   _____

10. huge, massive, monumental   _____

11. the universe, macrocosm, cosmos, totality   _____

12. to keep secret, withhold information   _____

13. a friendly chat; peace and quiet   _____

14. a correct usage   _____

Choosing the   *Circle the **boldface** word that more satisfactorily*
Right Word   *completes each of the following sentences.*

1. Please do not try to (**apprise, obfuscate**) your responsibility in this matter by irrelevant criticisms of other people's behavior.

2. Morality is not a criterion that can be used to judge whether or not a word belongs in a (**microcosm, lexicon**) of the language in which it is used.

3. I think it was very inconsiderate of her to wait until this late date before she (**apprised, obfuscated**) us of her intention to quit the class show.

4. Even the public opinion polls, which showed a strong trend toward our candidate, did not make us overly (**indigenous, sanguine**) about our chances of winning the primary.

5. At rush hour, I always have a hard time fighting my way through the (**melee, claque**) of tired commuters scurrying through the station.

6. Compared to today's free agents, the ballplayers of yesteryear were practically the (**lexicon, vassals**) of the team owners.

7. Falstaff, as conceived by Shakespeare, is not just a(n) (**lachrymose, bibulous**) old braggart but an archetype of human appetites and joy in living.

8. A basketball team will be sent to the Far East under the (**claque, aegis**) of the State Department to play native teams in various countries.

9. It is not enough merely to push aside our prejudices and pretend they don't exist; we must (**deracinate, apprise**) these evils from our minds and personalities.

10. From the observatory atop the World Trade Center, the pedestrians on the streets below look as (**sanguine, minuscule**) as atoms.

11. Under the American system of personal liberty, there are many aspects of day-to-day living that do not come within the (**claque, purview**) of any governmental authority.

12. In the tragedy that overtakes the pathetic Lennie in *Of Mice and Men*, we see in (**microcosm, purview**) the cruelty and injustice that pervade so many aspects of our society as a whole.

13. Their standards are so rigid and so devoid of a sense of proportion that they elevate every minor (**microcosm, solecism**) to the level of a major crime.

14. Is it any wonder that the young quarterback is getting a swelled head when he seems always to be surrounded by a(n) (**claque, aegis**) of admirers telling him how great he is?

15. In spite of the development of social security and insurance plans by the government, there is still a need for private (**minuscule, eleemosynary**) institutions to provide special services for needy people.

16. I came to resent the company's (**indigenous, paternalistic**) attitude because it assumed that the employees lacked the self-reliance or will power to take care of themselves.

17. The movie started off well, but the later scenes, with the beautiful young heroine slowly dying of cancer, became overwrought and (**bibulous, lachrymose**).

18. Those later scenes, in the opinion of many critics, had so much self-conscious pathos that they lacked conviction and (**verisimilitude, microcosm**).

19. For many years, there was a tendency on the part of both Americans and Europeans to ignore the highly developed (**lexical, indigenous**) cultures of the peoples of Africa.

20. If we disregard the emotions and desires of other groups in our local community, no matter how "unreasonable" we may consider them to be, we are simply going to increase partisanship and (**verisimilitude, polarization**).

Unit 3

Group A

ancillary	forte
bowdlerize	gratis
condescend	icon
cozen	interstice
enclave	macrocosm

Pronunciation   *Match each of the words contained in Group A with its phonetic transcription. Write the appropriate word in the space given.*

1. 'en klāv   _____

2. 'an sə ler ē   _____

3. 'mak rō koz əm   _____

4. fôrt *or* 'fôr tā   _____

5. 'ī kän   _____

6. 'bōd lə rīz   _____

7. 'kəz ən   _____

8. 'gra tis   _____

9. kon di 'send   _____

10. in 'tər stis   _____

Definition   *Choose the word from Group A that most nearly corresponds to each of the definitions below. Write the word in the blank space at the right of the definition and then in the illustrative phrase below it.*

1. (*v.*) to trick; to cheat or swindle   _____

_____ the unsuspecting tourist

2. (*n.*) the universe considered as a whole; the entire complex structure of something   _____

the economic _____

3. (*adj.*) subordinate or supplementary   _____

serve in a(n) _____ position

4. (*n.*) a small, narrow space between things or parts of things   _____

slipped through the _____

5. (*v.*) to remove material considered offensive (from a book, play, film, etc.)   _____

_____ the works of Shakespeare

6. (*n.*) a representation or image of a sacred personage, often considered sacred itself; an image or picture; a symbol; a graphic symbol on a computer monitor display; an object of blind devotion _____

an exhibition of Russian _____

7. (*n.*) an enclosed district, region, or area inhabited by a particular group of people or having a special character _____

a(n) _____ of resistance

8. (*n.*) a person's strong point; what a person does best _____

not my _____

9. (*v.*) to come down or stoop voluntarily to a lower level; to deal with people in a patronizing manner _____

_____ to speak to us

10. (*adj.*) free; (*adv.*) without charge _____

provided the service _____

Group B

mountebank
paean
persiflage
plethora
pragmatic

quizzical
rapacity
schism
therapeutic
virtuoso

Pronunciation   *Match each of the words contained in Group B with its phonetic transcription. Write the appropriate word in the space given.*

1. vər chü ′ō sō _____

2. ′kwiz i kəl _____

3. ′pē ən _____

4. ′maủn tə baŋk _____

5. rə ′pas ə tē _____

6. prag ′mat ik _____

7. ther ə ′pyü tik _____

8. ′pər sə fläzh _____

9. ′pleth ə rə _____

10. ′siz əm *or* ′skiz əm _____

3

Definition *Choose the word from Group B that most nearly corresponds to each of the definitions below. Write the word in the blank space to the right of the definition and then in the illustrative phrase below it.*

1. (*n.*) inordinate greed; the disposition to obtain one's desires by force, extortion, or plunder   _____

the _____ of a shark

2. (*n.*) a brilliant performer; a person with masterly skill or technique; (*adj.*) masterly or brilliant   _____

a great piano _____

3. (*n.*) a trickster or swindler; a charlatan   _____

nothing but a _____

4. (*n.*) a song of praise, joy, or triumph   _____

burst into a _____ of exultation

5. (*adj.*) having the power to heal or cure; beneficial   _____

the _____ effects of mineral water

6. (*adj.*) concerned with practical considerations or values; dealing with actions and results rather than with abstract theory   _____

a _____ approach to the problem

7. (*n.*) overfullness; superabundance; superfluity   _____

a _____ of questions

8. (*n.*) lighthearted joking, talk, or writing   _____

an endless flow of _____

9. (*n.*) a formal split within a religious organization; any division or separation of a group or organization into hostile factions   _____

a bitter _____

10. (*adj.*) puzzled; mocking; odd; equivocal   _____

a somewhat _____ expression on his face

Completing the Sentence *Choose the word for this unit that best completes each of the following sentences. Write it in the space given.*

1. When the soldiers realized that they had defeated the far more numerous

enemy, their cheers rose in a great _____ of jubilation and victory.

2. The "minor difference of opinion" developed into a(n) _____ that split the political party into two opposing factions.

3. His exaggerated claims for an expensive painkiller that turned out to be no more than aspirin exposed him as a(n) _____ .

4. The stubborn old-timers who refused to sell their homes came to form a(n) _____ of "natives" surrounded by "city people."

5. I would have welcomed any firm answer, no matter how unfavorable, but all that I got from her was a(n) _____ smile.

6. The coach used diagrams to show our receivers how to slip through the _____ in our opponent's zone pass coverage.

7. A good laugh invariably makes me feel better; I honestly believe that it has a(n) _____ effect on my disposition.

8. What point is there in dwelling on unproven theories when the problem we are facing demands that we be as _____ as possible?

9. At the height of Beatlemania in the mid-1960s the Fab Four assumed the stature of pop _____ .

10. In attempting to make the novel acceptable to the general public, the editor so _____ it that it lost its quality of stark realism.

11. Playing on his vanity and his desire to be known as a "good guy," I tried to _____ him into lending me his car.

12. When she neatly faked out the guard, pivoted, and drove in for a layup, I realized that I was seeing a true _____ on the basketball court.

13. The situation is growing worse because there is a(n) _____ of good intentions but a dearth of common sense and willingness to work hard.

14. To promote circulation, the publisher offered to throw in home delivery _____ for new subscribers to the Sunday edition.

15. My classmates selected me to address the community affairs committee because public speaking is a(n) _____ of mine.

16. He considers himself such a marvelous chess player that I'm surprised he would _____ to sit down at the board with a beginner like me.

17. Although we pride ourselves on the advance of civilization, the sad fact is that the _____ of 20th-century humanity has resulted in more destruction and suffering than ever before in history.

18. She thought of herself as a combination of Mark Twain and H. L. Mencken, but in my opinion her attempts at "devastating _____ " were abusive, coarse, and not very funny.

19. Once major matters like the advance and royalties had been settled, the publisher and agent negotiated whatever _____ rights were to be covered in the author's contract.

20. His self-importance stems from his inability to appreciate the very minor part he plays in the _____ of human affairs.

Synonyms   *Choose the word for this unit that is most nearly the **same** in meaning as each of the following groups of expressions. Write it in the space given.*

1. to stoop, deign, patronize   _____

2. a gap, slot, crevice, interval, lacuna   _____

3. an image, symbol, emblem; an idol   _____

4. an impostor, quack, charlatan, swindler   _____

5. banter, jesting, repartee, badinage   _____

6. avarice, greediness, cupidity, voraciousness   _____

7. to censor, purge, expurgate   _____

8. a hymn, ode, anthem   _____

9. an expert, master, prodigy, maestro   _____

10. free of charge, "on the house"; freely   _____

11. a gift, aptitude, specialty, strong suit   _____

12. curative, salutary, salubrious, beneficial   _____

13. a rift, breach, split in the ranks   _____

14. peculiar; perplexed, mystified; derisive   _____

15. practical, down-to-earth, businesslike   _____

16. a superfluity, surplus, surfeit, glut, excess   _____

17. to dupe, deceive; to beguile, inveigle   _____

18. auxiliary, subsidiary, accessory   _____

19. the universe, cosmos; an entirety   _____

20. an island, subgroup   _____

Antonyms *Choose the word for this unit that is most nearly **opposite** in meaning to each of the following groups of expressions. Write it in the space given.*

1. for a price _____

2. unequivocal, crystal-clear, unambiguous _____

3. a shortage, paucity, dearth, scarcity _____

4. a model, miniature, microcosm _____

5. idealistic, impractical, visionary _____

6. harmful, injurious, deleterious _____

7. central, key; primary, principal, main _____

8. a united front; a reconciliation _____

9. a weakness, shortcoming, foible _____

10. an amateur, beginner, novice; mediocre _____

11. a dirge, elegy, lament, threnody _____

12. liberality, generosity; altruism _____

13. a sucker, dupe, "mark," "pigeon" _____

Choosing the Right Word *Circle the **boldface** word that more satisfactorily completes each of the following sentences.*

1. The first serious (**schism, enclave**) in the Communist world of the postwar era occurred in 1948, when Yugoslavia began in earnest to distance itself from the Soviet Union.

2. It is a common mistake to assume that shrewdness in business affairs must be accompanied by extreme (**rapacity, mountebank**).

3. Simply because we have dropped a few objectionable words from the dialogue does not justify the critic's statement that we have (**cozened, bowdlerized**) the play.

4. Our little group of would-be writers, painters, and musicians formed an (**enclave, ancillary**) of culture in what we considered a hostile world.

5. After the great victory his quiet and modest statements were far more impressive than the most effusive (**paean, interstice**) could have been.

6. They can't force you to do anything, but it is quite possible that they will be able to (**condescend, cozen**) you into actions against your best interests.

7. In this situation, when I desperately needed material help, I was deluged with a(n) (**plethora, enclave**) of glib and gratuitous advice.

8. A theory that seems valid in the confines of a small family group may be proved useless when applied in the (**macrocosm, interstice**) of society at large.

9. In the great crises of life, you must depend basically on yourself; the help you get from others can only be (**pragmatic, ancillary**).

10. A political candidate who promises to solve all our social problems without ever mentioning greater expenditures and higher taxes would certainly be dismissed as a (**mountebank, schism**).

11. Though acupuncture has been practiced in Eastern medicine for centuries, its (**therapeutic, quizzical**) value has only recently been acknowledged by doctors in the West.

12. The clash of wits between those two brilliant columnists was no mere (**persiflage, paean**), but an exchange of deadly insults.

13. The sun left its mottled imprint on the wall as the rays filtered through the (**enclaves, interstices**) of the iron grating.

14. A truly great leader must possess both the inspiration of a visionary and the (**quizzical, pragmatic**) skills of an experienced politician.

15. In sandpainting, an art still practiced by the Navajos and Pueblos of the American Southwest, designs are created of (**icons, fortes**) representing animals, deities, and natural phenomena.

16. Her easygoing attitude and resilience, far from being a weakness, proved to be her (**mountebank, forte**) in surviving during that trying period.

17. If, as they say, they find those people so vulgar and unpleasant, why do they (**cozen, condescend**) to associate with them?

18. Because he sees life as a pattern of ambiguities and contradictions, he likes to express himself in the form of (**quizzical, ancillary**) witticisms.

19. The dictum "There's no such thing as a free lunch" means that nothing worthwhile in life comes to us (**forte, gratis**).

20. Your (**virtuosity, pragmatism**) as a public speaker and campaigner may earn you votes, but it cannot make up for your lack of experience and knowledge of public affairs.

Analogies   *In each of the following, choose the item that best completes the comparison.*

1. aegis is to **protection** as
a. hierarchy is to experience
b. maelstrom is to sanctuary
c. vignette is to encouragement
d. buttress is to support

2. bibulous is to **drink** as
a. rapacious is to clothing
b. gluttonous is to food
c. altruistic is to money
d. vegetarian is to meat

3. bowdlerize is to **out** as
a. abbreviate is to in
b. annotate is to out
c. interpolate is to in
d. duplicate is to out

4. oblivious is to **awareness** as
a. comatose is to consciousness
b. serene is to composure
c. erudite is to knowledge
d. adroit is to skill

5. obfuscate is to **clarity** as
a. illuminate is to light
b. deracinate is to precision
c. invigorate is to energy
d. adulterate is to purity

6. poltroon is to **pusillanimous** as
a. jester is to lachrymose
b. dynamo is to supine
c. optimist is to sanguine
d. progressive is to hidebound

7. mirage is to **illusory** as
a. will-o'-the-wisp is to elusive
b. thunderclap is to noisome
c. rainbow is to chimerical
d. eclipse is to luminous

8. schism is to **polarize** as
a. controversy is to reconcile
b. merger is to unite
c. covenant is to antagonize
d. compromise is to estrange

9. mountebank is to **cozen** as
a. turncoat is to cheat
b. panhandler is to kill
c. embezzler is to abduct
d. highwayman is to rob

10. bellwether is to **barometer** as
a. proselyte is to spark plug
b. cynosure is to magnet
c. morass is to catalyst
d. liturgy is to lightning rod

Identification   *In each of the following groups, circle the word that is best defined or suggested by the introductory phrase.*

1. how one might characterize the Everglades
a. bellwether   b. liturgy   c. morass   d. mirage

2. "It's no use crying over spilled milk."
a. hierarchy   b. fait accompli   c. poltroon   d. vignette

3. These plants have always grown here.
a. bibulous   b. sanguine   c. indigenous   d. eleemosynary

4. a person's "long suit"
a. interstice   b. gratis   c. therapeutic   d. forte

5. The instincts of a "shark"
a. rapacity   b. virtuoso   c. melee   d. raillery

6. I always do it that way and no other way!
a. quasi   b. effete   c. hidebound   d. obfuscate

7. completely absorbed in a daydream
a. oblivious   b. virtuoso   c. pragmatic   d. noisome

8. reading a book while lying on the lounge
a. ribald   b. supine   c. cozen   d. deracinate

9. how one might characterize a tearjerker
a. lachrymose   b. polarized   c. quizzical   d. ancillary

10. It's hardly worth bothering about
a. macrocosm   b. minuscule   c. condescend   d. rapacity

11. I'm glad I done it!
a. purview   b. verisimilitude   c. aegis   d. solecism

12. The chairperson brought the committee up to date on the new developments.
a. apprise   b. caterwaul   c. deter   d. bowdlerize

13. He certainly fooled us!
a. proselyte   b. mountebank   c. schism   d. pragmatist

14. delighted to listen to their clever give-and-take
a. persiflage   b. paean   c. lexicon   d. paternalism

Shades of Meaning   *Read each sentence carefully. Then encircle the item that best completes the sentence below it.*

Attached to units of the Red Army were political commissars, Communist party ideologues whose pragmatic and tyrannical ways made them the (2) objects of fear and contempt on the part of the common soldiers.

1. The word **pragmatic** in line 2 most nearly means
a. practical   b. businesslike   c. doctrinaire   d. conspiratorial

Adopting the role of virtuoso, newspaper magnate William Randolph Hearst scoured Europe in the 1920s for antiques and objets d'art with (2) which to furnish San Simeon, his immense California estate.

2. In line 1 the word **virtuoso** is used to mean
a. maestro   b. prodigy   c. tycoon   d. connoisseur

Abraham Lincoln's keen sense of humor and his willingness to make fun of himself are among the adjuncts that have endeared him to the (2) American public.

3. The best definition for the word **adjuncts** in line 2 is
a. qualities   b. associates   c. subordinates   d. accessories

"This fellow here with envious carping tongue
Upbraided me about the rose I wear, (2)
Saying the sanguine color of the leaves
Did represent my master's blushing cheeks . . ." (4)
     (Shakespeare, 1 *Henry VI,* IV, 1, 90–93)

4. In line 3 the word **sanguine** most nearly means
a. cheerful   b. red   c. optimistic   d. confident

Despite the claims advanced in commercials, I find it hard to believe that one brand of paper towel is more bibulous than another. (2)

5. The best definition for the word **bibulous** in line 2 is
a. absorbent   c. fond of the bottle
b. inebrious   d. soft

28

Antonyms   *In each of the following groups, circle the word or expression that is most nearly **opposite** in meaning to the first word in **boldface type**.*

1. chimerical
a. impossible
b. fortunate
c. comprehensive
d. realistic

2. obfuscate
a. bedim
b. exemplify
c. clarify
d. slander

3. oblivious
a. thankful
b. tolerant
c. smug
d. cognizant

4. therapeutic
a. curative
b. injurious
c. medicinal
d. practical

5. sanguine
a. bloody
b. obvious
c. tasteless
d. gloomy

6. noisome
a. wholesome
b. quiet
c. tasty
d. loathsome

7. pragmatic
a. earthy
b. prominent
c. idealistic
d. inquisitive

8. hidebound
a. tough
b. progressive
c. soft
d. prone

9. deracinate
a. implant
b. twist
c. conceal
d. flourish

10. indigenous
a. modern
b. alien
c. ornamental
d. natural

11. effete
a. vigorous
b. exhausted
c. lax
d. awkward

12. bibulous
a. limited
b. sedate
c. abstemious
d. convivial

13. paean
a. lament
b. sonnet
c. soliloquy
d. duet

14. deracinate
a. uproot
b. solve
c. implant
d. appear

15. plethora
a. surfeit
b. dearth
c. contrast
d. supply

16. poltroon
a. follower
b. stalwart
c. milksop
d. employer

17. quizzical
a. amused
b. unequivocal
c. contorted
d. dissimilar

18. polarize
a. explore
b. split
c. weatherize
d. unify

19. ancillary
a. dependent
b. concomitant
c. relevant
d. primary

20. schism
a. reconciliation
b. compartment
c. regulation
d. buffet

Completing the Sentence   *From the following list of words, choose the one that best completes each of the sentences below. Write the word in the space provided.*

interstice
rapacity

macrocosm
condescend

cozen
sanguine

hierarchy
quasi-

1. I was amazed that the august senior would _____ to allow me to drive him home.

2. Helen soon learned to fill the _____ between the intense workouts with relaxation exercises.

3. Ben quickly learned his lowly place in the _____ of employees in the busy supermarket.

4. Will Earth be able to survive the _____ of humanity in the name of progress?

R

5. How could you have allowed them to _____ you into voting for their ticket?

6. Even a person of his _____ temperament could not maintain his optimism in the face of such a series of misfortunes.

Interesting Derivations   *From the following list of words, choose the one that best completes each of the sentences below. Write the word in the space provided.*

aegis	**plethora**	**lexicon**	**chimerical**
claque	**bowdlerize**	**paean**	**proselyte**

1. The name of the early 19th-century English editor who rigorously excised "questionable" words, phrases, lines, and scenes from his "family edition" of Shakespeare's plays is remembered in the verb _____ .

2. The goatskin shield or breastplate bearing the head of Medusa and used by Zeus and Athena is the source of the English noun _____ .

3. One of the many epithets of Apollo, the god of music, poetry, and the arts, is the basis for the English noun _____ .

4. The fire-breathing mythological monster with the head and forepaws of a lion, the body and hind legs of a goat, and the tail of a dragon is the source of the English adjective _____ .

Word Families

A. *On the line provided, write a **noun form** for each of the following words.*

EXAMPLE: obfuscate—**obfuscation**

1. chimerical   _____
2. oblivious   _____
3. ribald   _____
4. pragmatic   _____
5. therapeutic   _____
6. indigenous   _____
7. deracinate   _____
8. polarize   _____
9. condescend   _____
10. lachrymose   _____
11. bowdlerize   _____

B. *On the line provided, write an **adjective** related to each of the following words.*

EXAMPLE: lexicon—**lexical**

1. hierarchy _____

2. icon _____

3. liturgy _____

4. paternalism _____

5. rapacity _____

6. verisimilitude _____

Filling the Blanks   *Encircle the pair of words that best complete the meaning of each of the following passages.*

1. The social structure of the South in the days before the Civil War was rigidly _____ , with the gentleman planter at the summit of the edifice and the chattel slave at its base. _____ notions of caste discouraged whites from moving freely within the system, and the "peculiar institution" denied blacks any mobility whatsoever.

a. pragmatic . . . Polarized
b. hierarchical . . . Hidebound
c. therapeutic . . . Cozened
d. chimerical . . . Obfuscated

2. As the detachment of knights galloped over the crest of the hill, it collided with a column of enemy foot soldiers moving up the other side. In the brief but bloody _____ that ensued, two of the king's most prominent _____ lost their lives, and the Duke of Orleans was wounded.

a. schism . . . proselytes
b. purview . . . mountebanks
c. melee . . . vassals
d. vignette . . . bellwethers

3. On more than one occasion during the Middle Ages, controversy about some point of doctrine _____ ecclesiastical opinion and produced a temporary _____ in the Christian church.

a. polarized . . . schism
b. bowdlerized . . . fait accompli
c. obfuscated . . . enclave
d. deracinated . . . macrocosm

4. Your composition is so full of _____ , malapropisms, and general gobbledygook that I suggest you study a grammar book, a _____ , and a style manual before you ever again put pen to paper.

a. interstices . . . liturgy
b. raillery . . . microcosm
c. persiflage . . . plethora
d. solecisms . . . lexicon

Unit 4

Group A

affinity	**derring-do**
bilious	**divination**
cognate	**elixir**
corollary	**folderol**
cul-de-sac	**gamut**

Pronunciation *Match each of the words contained in Group A with its phonetic transcription. Write the appropriate word in the space given.*

1. 'gam ət _____

2. 'der iŋ dü _____

3. 'kog nāt _____

4. ə 'fin ə tē _____

5. 'fol də rol _____

6. i 'lik sər _____

7. 'kəl də sak _____

8. div ə 'nā shən _____

9. 'bil yəs _____

10. 'kôr ə ler ē _____

Definition *Choose the word from Group A that most nearly corresponds to each of the definitions below. Write the word in the blank space at the right of the definition and then in the illustrative phrase below it.*

1. (*n.*) an entire range or series _____

   ran the _____ from praise to scorn

2. (*n.*) valor or heroism; daring deeds or exploits (often used to poke fun at false heroics) _____

   breathtaking feats of _____

3. (*n.*) a natural attraction to a person, thing, or activity; a relationship, connection _____

   a mysterious _____ between them

4. (*n.*) a proposition that follows from one already proven; a natural consequence or result; (*adj.*) resultant or consequent _____

   an axiom and its _____

5. (*adj.*) peevish or irritable; sickeningly unpleasant _____

   a(n) _____ shade of green

6. (*n.*) foolish talk, ideas, or procedures; nonsense; a trifle   _____

    won't put up with such _____

7. (*adj.*) closely related in origin, essential nature, or function; (*n.*) such a person or thing   _____

    _____ words like *pater* and *father*

8. (*n.*) a potion once thought capable of curing all ills and maintaining life indefinitely; a panacea; a sweet liquid used as a vehicle in medicines   _____

    the _____ of life

9. (*n.*) a blind alley or dead-end street; any situation in which further progress is impossible; an impasse   _____

    trapped in a hopeless _____

10. (*n.*) the art or act of predicting the future or discovering hidden knowledge   _____

    skilled in _____

Group B

hoi polloi	**parameter**
ineffable	**pundit**
lucubration	**risible**
mnemonic	**symptomatic**
obloquy	**volte-face**

Pronunciation   *Match each of the words contained in Group B with its phonetic transcription. Write the appropriate word in the space given.*

1. ni ′mon ik   _____

2. pə ′ram ə tər   _____

3. volt ′fäs   _____

4. ′riz ə bəl   _____

5. hoi pə ′loi   _____

6. ′pən dit   _____

7. lü kyù ′brā shən   _____

8. simp tə ′mat ik   _____

9. ′ob lə kwē   _____

10. in ′ef ə bəl   _____

4

Definition Choose the word from Group B that most nearly corresponds to each of the definitions below. Write the word in the blank space to the right of the definition and then in the illustrative phrase below it.

1. (*adj.*) pertaining to laughter; able or inclined to laugh; laughable _____

the _____ antics of a clown

2. (*n.*) the common people, the masses _____

catering to the _____

3. (*n.*) public abuse indicating strong disapproval or censure; the disgrace resulting from such treatment _____

heaped _____ on the head of the offending official

4. (*adj.*) typical or characteristic; being or concerned with a symptom of a disease _____

a condition _____ of decline

5. (*n.*) an about-face; a complete reversal _____

a totally unexpected _____

6. (*adj.*) not expressible in words; too great or too sacred to be uttered _____

the _____ joy of parenthood

7. (*adj.*) relating to or designed to assist the memory; (*n.*) a device to aid the memory _____

phenomenal _____ skills

8. (*n.*) laborious study or thought, especially at night; the result of such work _____

the _____ of a scholar

9. (*n.*) a determining or characteristic element; a factor that shapes the total outcome; a limit, boundary _____

analyze the _____ of the nation's military potential

10. (*n.*) a learned person; one who gives authoritative opinions _____

a renowned _____ of the theater

Completing the Sentence Choose the word for this unit that best completes each of the following sentences. Write it in the space given.

1. Foreign visitors sometimes dismiss our national political conventions as

mere _____ because they do not appreciate the serious political work being done beneath the surface pageantry.

2. This short sentence will serve as a(n) _____ to help you remember the names of the first eight Presidents: "*Will A Jolly Man Make A Jolly Visitor?*"

3. After having strongly supported the teaching of foreign languages, they made a complete _____ and advocated that this part of the curriculum be dropped or limited to a small minority.

4. The relief we felt when we realized they were safe was so profound and overwhelming as to be utterly _____ .

5. The lecturer said that the soaring crime statistics are _____ of a society in which traditional values and standards are breaking down.

6. The role calls for an actor who can express a(n) _____ of emotions, from speechless rage to utter bliss.

7. The _____ tenor of the remarks that they offered to us as "constructive criticism" betrayed just how sorely they envied our success.

8. Your ponderous _____ seemed to me intended much more to emphasize your own brilliance and importance than to shed any real light on the subject.

9. The situation calls for courage, in the sense of a sustained, resolute, and patient effort—not occasional feats of _____ .

10. Having been maneuvered into a(n) _____ , the retreating troops could do nothing but turn and fight a battle for survival against superior forces.

11. In a truly democratic society, there are no sharp differences in status and privilege between self-styled aristocrats and the _____ .

12. In estimating the relative military strength of the two powers, we must concentrate on the _____ by which ability to carry on modern warfare may be judged.

13. Is our blind faith in computerized analysis any different in its essentials from the belief of so-called primitive peoples in _____ ?

14. The intensive merchandising and tremendous sale of patent medicines shows that mankind has never really ceased its search for an all-purpose _____ .

15. All kittens display a natural _____ for mischief, but I have never known one so bent on monkey business as our Mickie.

16. No sooner did the press conference end than the network correspondent turned to a group of political _____ for an instant analysis of the President's performance.

17. The suggestion was so _____ that I couldn't help laughing out loud as soon as I heard it.

18. In reading a passage in French or Spanish, I can often guess the meanings of many words I have never seen before, because they are all recognizable _____ of familiar English words.

19. I know that they deserve to be condemned, but I can't bring myself to heap _____ on them when they are in such a state of disgrace and humilation.

20. It is true that capital punishment has not been proved to be a deterrent to murder, but it would be invalid to draw from this the _____ that it has been proved *not* to be a deterrent.

Synonyms   *Choose the word for this unit that is most nearly the* ***same*** *in meaning as each of the following groups of expressions. Write it in the space given.*

1. droll, ludicrous, laughable _____

2. indicative, typical, characteristic _____

3. an attraction, inclination, penchant _____

4. prophecy, prediction, augury _____

5. allied, affiliated, related; a relative _____

6. discredit, opprobrium, ignominy, dishonor _____

7. inexpressible, indescribable _____

8. a turnabout, reversal, about-face _____

9. hoopla; gibberish, nonsense _____

10. a panacea, cure-all, nostrum, tonic _____

11. a dead end, blind alley, impasse _____

12. a deduction, conclusion _____

13. burning the midnight oil, deep thought _____

14. choleric, irascible, peevish, splenetic _____

15. an expert, authority, savant _____

16. scope, compass, sweep, range _____

17. the rank and file, masses _____

18. a factor, limit, boundary _____

19. audacity, bravado, pyrotechnics   _____

20. a reminder, cue, memory aid   _____

Antonyms   _Choose the word for this unit that is most nearly **opposite** in meaning to each of the following groups of expressions. Write it in the space given._

1. an axiom, postulate, premise   _____

2. a distaste, aversion   _____

3. praise, acclaim, approbation   _____

4. cowardice, timidity, poltroonery   _____

5. the aristocracy, elite, upper class   _____

6. dissimilar, unrelated   _____

7. sweet-tempered, genial; pleasant, delightful   _____

8. depressing; poignant, heartrending   _____

9. a layman, amateur, dilettante   _____

10. sense, significance   _____

Choosing the Right Word   _Circle the **boldface** word that more satisfactorily completes each of the following sentences._

1. The devastating stock market crash of 1929 surprised not only laymen, but Wall Street (**corollaries, pundits**) as well.

2. In an age of genocide, atomic weapons, and threats of ecological disaster, do you really expect a sensible person to be fascinated by such romantic tales of (**parameters, derring-do**)?

3. I know that you have had many difficulties and disappointments in life, but I fail to see how you are helping either yourself or others by behaving in such a (**bilious, cognate**) and offensive manner.

4. In the _Inferno_, Dante introduces personages from history and mythology to portray the full (**gamut, folderol**) of human folly and wickedness.

5. Your irresponsible behavior has finally caught up with you; you are in a(n) (**cul-de-sac, hoi polloi**) from which it will be all but impossible to extricate yourself.

6. The first thing we must do is establish the (**parameters, lucubrations**) of the problem, so that we can begin to think in terms of a practical solution.

7. We must expect to see politicians modify their programs and points of view from time to time, but a sudden, unexpected (**cognate, volte-face**) by a candidate on a crucial issue is more than we can tolerate.

8. Henry had an excellent chance to make an honorable career for himself, but he seemed to have a fatal (**affinity, corollary**) for easy money and shady deals.

9. Those remarkably accurate predictions were based not on (**lucubration, divination**) but on insight into human nature and a sound understanding of the objective elements in the situation.

10. Many sociologists believe that the high divorce rate in the United States is (**symptomatic, ineffable**) of basic strains and flaws in our social structure.

11. The advice which they offered us with such pretentious solemnity turned out to be a tissue of platitudes and (**folderol, elixir**).

12. We found it more difficult to master the (**mnemonic, parameter**) than it would have been to memorize the material to which it was keyed.

13. It is little short of incredible that all their mountainous (**lucubrations, divinations**) have brought forth that tiny mouse of an idea.

14. I knew that if I ran for public office, I would be exposed to severe criticism, but I never expected such a flood of (**obloquy, elixir**).

15. No student of anthropology can fail to recognize the (**cognate, corollary**) elements in the cultures of societies which seem, at first glance, to be vastly different from one another.

16. I have listened to their eloquent demonstration that the present situation is hopeless, but I am unwilling to accept the (**gamut, corollary**) that the only course left open to us is craven surrender.

17. The pithy comments of that brilliant and delightful woman were a(n) (**elixir, cul-de-sac**) that we found extraordinarily exhilarating.

18. It may seem to be a paradox, but I believe it is true that only a basically serious person can fully appreciate the (**risible, bilious**) factors in life.

19. Only a supreme actor could express so eloquently the (**risible, ineffable**) quality of the "thoughts that do often lie too deep for tears."

20. Is your repeated use of the expression (**cul-de-sac, hoi polloi**) supposed to convey the idea that you are not one of the people?

Group A

aficionado	foray
browbeat	genre
commensurate	homily
diaphanous	immure
emolument	insouciant

Pronunciation *Match each of the words contained in Group A with its phonetic transcription. Write the appropriate word in the space given.*

1. i 'myür _____

2. i 'mol yə mənt _____

3. 'braủ bēt _____

4. 'fôr ā _____

5. ə fish yə 'nä dō _____

6. in 'sü sē ənt _____

7. 'hom ə lē _____

8. dī 'af ə nəs _____

9. 'zhän rə _____

10. kə 'men sə rit _____

Definition *Choose the word from Group A that most nearly corresponds to each of the definitions below. Write the word in the blank space at the right of the definition and then in the illustrative phrase below it.*

1. (*n.*) a sermon stressing moral principles; a tedious moralizing lecture or discourse _____

　　　a Sunday-morning _____

2. (*n.*) an enthusiastic and usually expert follower or fan _____

　　　a(n) _____ of the game since my youth

3. (*n.*) a quick raid, especially for plunder; a venture into some field of endeavor; (*v.*) to make such a raid _____

　　　a successful _____ behind the enemy's lines

4. (*adj.*) blithely indifferent or unconcerned; carefree; happy-go-lucky _____

　　　a(n) _____ attitude to life

5. (*v.*) to intimidate by a stern or overbearing manner; to bully   _____

   _____ them into agreeing

6. (*n.*) profit derived from an office or position or from employment; a fee or salary   _____

   an equitable _____

7. (*v.*) to enclose or confine within walls; to imprison; to seclude or isolate   _____

   _____ for life in a narrow cell

8. (*adj.*) equal in size, extent, duration, or importance; proportionate; measurable by the same standards   _____

   rewards _____ with their efforts

9. (*adj.*) very sheer and light; almost completely transparent   _____

   a(n) _____ material like gauze

10. (*n.*) a type, class, or variety, especially a distinctive category of literary composition; a style of painting in which everyday scenes are realistically depicted   _____

   the sci-fi _____

Group B

matrix	**prurient**
obsequies	**sacrosanct**
panache	**systemic**
persona	**tendentious**
philippic	**vicissitude**

Pronunciation   *Match each of the words contained in Group B with its phonetic transcription. Write the appropriate word in the space given.*

1. ten 'den shəs   _____

2. 'ob sə kwēz   _____

3. pər 'sō nə   _____

4. pə 'nash   _____

5. vi 'sis ə tüd   _____

6. sis 'tem ik   _____

7. 'mā triks   _____

8. 'sak rō saŋkt   _____

9. fi 'lip ik   _____

10. 'prủr ē ənt   _____

Definition   *Choose the word from Group B that most nearly
corresponds to each of the definitions below. Write the
word in the blank space at the right of the definition and
then in the illustrative phrase below it.*

1. (*adj.*) very sacred or holy; inviolable; set apart or
immune from questioning or attack   _____

a(n) _____ relic

2. (*n.*) a change, variation, or alteration; (*pl.*) successive
or changing phases or conditions   _____

the inevitable _____ of life

3. (*n.*) a mold; the surrounding situation or environment   _____

a wax _____

4. (*adj.*) of or pertaining to the entire body; relating to a
system or systems   _____

a(n) _____ breakdown

5. (*n.*) funeral rites or ceremonies   _____

held impressive _____ for their leader

6. (*adj.*) intended to promote a particular point of view,
doctrine, or cause; biased or partisan   _____

a(n) _____ argument

7. (*n.*) a character in a novel or play; the outward
character or role that a person assumes   _____

a comic _____

8. (*n.*) a confident and stylish manner, dash; a strikingly
elaborate or colorful display   _____

the _____ of the knights of old

9. (*adj.*) having lustful desires or interests; tending to
arouse sexual desires   _____

a(n) _____ novel

10. (*n.*) a bitter verbal attack   _____

a searing _____ against the proposal

**Completing
the Sentence**   *Choose the word for this unit that best completes each
of the following sentences. Write it in the space given.*

1. It was a cat-and-mouse play of a patient detective and an aristocratic jewel

thief who stole with elegance and _____ .

2. Our troops returned from their successful _____ against the
enemy's base in a jubilant mood.

3. In her speech to the entering freshman class, the dean emphasized that the benefits they derived from any course would be _____ with the effort that they devoted to it.

4. When doctors discovered the disease to be _____ , they held out little hope for the patient's recovery.

5. At first she showed only a mild interest in bridge, but as she played more and developed skill, she became a real _____ of the game.

6. Having been conditioned as children to take wealth and luxury for granted, they tended to take a(n) _____ attitude toward money, even when they had only a modest income.

7. In my opinion, the epic poem represents the most noble and inspiring of all literary _____ .

8. You should not approach a class in sex education with such a leering and _____ attitude.

9. What good does it do to regale the prisoners with _____ about "going straight" if they have no chance to make an honest living when they are released?

10. She claimed to be an unbiased witness, but I found her testimony to be opinionated and _____ .

11. We found overwhelming beauty in the most common manifestations of nature, such as the colors of sunset, the delicate shape of a flower, or the _____ wings of an insect.

12. She cannot relate to other people in a constructive way because she is _____ in her own prejudices and hostilities.

13. When we reflected on his long and happy life and his unmatched record of public service, we found the _____ comforting and even inspiring, rather than depressing.

14. One of my fondest hopes is to visit Jerusalem, the city that has had a unique role in history as the _____ of three great world religions.

15. The overbearing maitre d' _____ the diners into meekly accepting the least desirable table in the restaurant.

16. The Constitution provides that the _____ received by the President is to be neither increased nor decreased during his term of office.

17. Their reverence for all creations of God was so great that, in their eyes, even the most common manifestation of nature was _____ .

18. The true test of her character will be how she is able to deal with the

_____ of life.

19. Time after time, he rose on the floor of the Senate and delivered bitter

_____ against the lack of effective measures against
environmental pollution.

20. The omniscient narrator is probably the most common _____
assumed by novel writers.

Synonyms   *Choose the word for this unit that is most nearly the
same in meaning as each of the following groups of
expressions. Write it in the space given.*

1. extensive, comprehensive, system-wide   _____

2. a sermon, lecture, discourse   _____

3. a salary, pay, wages, compensation   _____

4. a devotee, enthusiast, fan, follower   _____

5. nonchalant, blasé, devil-may-care   _____

6. translucent, sheer, gossamer   _____

7. partisan, biased, partial   _____

8. a fluctuation, vacillation   _____

9. lascivious, salacious, lewd, titillating   _____

10. a sally, raid, sortie   _____

11. to incarcerate, mew up, imprison   _____

12. a harangue, tirade, diatribe   _____

13. style, verve, élan, éclat, flamboyance   _____

14. a personality, image, role   _____

15. sacred, inviolable   _____

16. comparable, corresponding, coordinate   _____

17. a species, sort, variety, class, school   _____

18. to intimidate, cow, bully, coerce   _____

19. a mold, pattern, model; an environment   _____

20. last rites, funeral services   _____

5

Antonyms *Choose the word for this unit that is most nearly **opposite** in meaning to each of the following groups of expressions. Write it in the space given.*

1. opaque; coarse, dense _____

2. to release, liberate, emancipate _____

3. fair, impartial, equitable, disinterested _____

4. an encomium, panegyric, tribute _____

5. worried, careworn, agitated, distraught _____

6. a sameness, evenness, lack of change _____

7. a retreat, strategic withdrawal _____

8. prudish, demure, innocent _____

9. a lack of pizzazz or style _____

10. localized, specific, isolated, confined _____

11. to coax, cajole, wheedle, sweet-talk _____

Choosing the Right Word *Circle the **boldface** word that more satisfactorily completes each of the following sentences.*

1. The purpose of our policies is to develop bold new forms of international understanding and practical cooperation that can serve as the (**philippic, matrix**) for a stable peace.

2. Young people involved in drug abuse need practical help in overcoming their addiction—not (**homilies, obsequies**) exhorting them to higher standards of behavior.

3. Corot painted poetic and (**diaphanous, tendentious**) landscapes, in which even solid objects seemed to be suffused with light and movement.

4. If the woman thinks her status as a public official renders her (**insouciant, sacrosanct**), she is in for a rude awakening.

5. James Bond seems to dispose of the villains he faces with all the (**genre, panache**) of the legendary paladins of medieval romance.

6. The (**matrix, persona**) that a public figure displays to the world is often quite different from the personality that he or she exhibits in private.

7. It seems almost incredible to us today that a few generations ago a novel of such quality could be widely condemned as vulgar, salacious, and designed to appeal to (**tendentious, prurient**) interests.

8. We do not believe in guilt by association, but certainly your judgment, if not your motives, must be questioned when you choose to associate yourself with an organization of that (**matrix, genre**).

9. How can young people hope to become mature, self-reliant adults if they (**immure, foray**) themselves in a home environment that is so comfortable and protective?

10. It is often said that in the Soviet Union there are as many (**vicissitudes, aficionados**) of chess as there are of baseball or golf in the United States.

11. I had hoped to hear a balanced, dispassionate discussion of this problem, but I found their approach to be distressingly one-sided and (**tendentious, sacrosanct**).

12. The commission found that police corruption was not confined to one or two isolated precincts but was (**systemic, prurient**) in nature.

13. I admit that you have some grounds for complaint, but those shrieks of outrage are simply not (**diaphanous, commensurate**) with having been overcharged five cents.

14. The fact that they referred to my salary as a(n) (**panache, emolument**) did not disguise the fact that I was being woefully underpaid.

15. The defense attorney claimed that the police had used scare tactics to (**browbeat, foray**) her client into a confession.

16. What gourmet feast can compare with the luscious delicacies that we consumed during our midnight (**forays, homilies**) on the well-stocked refrigerator?

17. What we owe to our fallen leader is not mournful (**philippics, obsequies**), but a joyful assertion of life and a pledge to continue her work.

18. The Bible reminds us that even in moments of great joy we should retain some awareness of the (**panache, vicissitudes**) and heartbreaks of life.

19. When the results of the scholarship competition were announced, we could sense the deep disappointment beneath your (**insouciant, tendentious**) manner.

20. There is no doubt of your oratorical talents, but this is a time for quiet words of reconciliation—not for thundering (**emoluments, philippics**).

Unit 6

Group A

abortive	iconoclastic
bruit	in medias res
contumelious	internecine
dictum	maladroit
ensconce	maudlin

Pronunciation *Match each of the words contained in Group A with its phonetic transcription. Write the appropriate word in the space given.*

1. int ər 'nes ēn _____

2. ə 'bôr tiv _____

3. 'dik təm _____

4. 'môd lin _____

5. kon tü 'mē lē əs _____

6. in 'med ē əs 'rās _____

7. brüt _____

8. mal ə 'droit _____

9. en 'skons _____

10. ī kon ə 'klas tik _____

Definition *Choose the word from Group A that most nearly corresponds to each of the following definitions. Write the word in the blank space at the right of the definition and then in the illustrative phrase below it.*

1. (*adj.*) mutually destructive; characterized by great slaughter and bloodshed _____

a(n) _____ feud

2. (*adj.*) failing to accomplish an intended aim or purpose; only partially or imperfectly developed _____

a(n) _____ attempt to seize the throne

3. (*adv.*) in or into the middle of a plot; into the middle of things _____

since the poem begins _____

4. (*adj.*) lacking skill or dexterity; lacking tact, perception, or judgment _____

their _____ interference

5. (*adj.*) excessively or effusively sentimental _____

a(n) _____ ditty

6. (*v.*) to spread news, reports, or unsubstantiated rumors

                _____

    was immediately _____ about the town

7. (*v.*) to settle comfortably and firmly in position; to put or hide in a safe place

                _____

    happily _____ in a snug, warm bed

8. (*adj.*) attacking or seeking to overthrow popular or traditional beliefs, ideas, or institutions

                _____

    _____ opinions

9. (*adj.*) insolent or rude in speech or behavior; insultingly abusive; humiliating

                _____

    a(n)˚_____ reply

10. (*n.*) a short saying; an authoritative statement

                _____

    according to the _____ of the critics

Group B

modulate	**saturnalian**
portentous	**touchstone**
prescience	**traumatic**
quid pro quo	**vitiate**
salubrious	**waggish**

Pronunciation   *Match each of the words contained in Group B with its phonetic transcription. Write the appropriate word in the space given.*

1. pôr ′ten təs   _____

2. ′wag ish   _____

3. ′presh əns   _____

4. ′mod yə lāt   _____

5. trau ′mat ik   _____

6. ′vish ē āt   _____

7. sat ər ′nā lyan   _____

8. ′kwid prō ′kwō   _____

9. ′təch stōn   _____

10. sə ′lü brē əs   _____

Definition   *Choose the word from Group B that most nearly corresponds to each of the following definitions. Write the word in the blank space at the right of the definition and then in the illustrative phrase below it.*

1. (*adj.*) fond of making jokes; characteristic of a joker; playfully humorous or droll   _____

amused by her _____ remarks

2. (*n.*) knowledge of events or actions before they happen; foresight   _____

amazed by his _____

3. (*adj.*) characterized by riotous or unrestrained revelry or licentiousness   _____

a boisterously _____ spectacle

4. (*adj.*) foreshadowing an event to come; causing wonder or awe; self-consciously weighty, pompous   _____

a(n) _____ style

5. (*adj.*) conducive to health or well-being; wholesome   _____

the _____ effects of sea air

6. (*n.*) a means of testing worth or genuineness   _____

a(n) _____ of literary merit

7. (*v.*) to change or vary the intensity or pitch; to temper or soften; to regulate, adjust   _____

_____ their voices

8. (*n.*) something given in exchange or return for something else   _____

insisted on some _____

9. (*v.*) to weaken, debase, or corrupt; to impair the quality or value of   _____

_____ by our lack of managerial skill

10. (*adj.*) so shocking to the emotions as to cause lasting and substantial psychological damage   _____

a thoroughly _____ experience

Completing the Sentence   *Choose the word for this unit that best completes each of the following sentences. Write it in the space given.*

1. Though the guests at the gala benefit tried to maintain an air of cheer, the

_____ news of the international crisis hung like a pall over the gathering.

2. For many years, Churchill's warnings about Hitler were dismissed as "alarmism"; only after the outbreak of World War II did his countrymen appreciate his extraordinary _____ .

3. More than anything else, the ability to create distinctive characters and make them "come alive" on the page is the _____ of a great novelist.

4. The coach devised a clever strategy, but it proved _____ when our team failed to execute it properly.

5. How can you expect them to cooperate with us unless they receive some reasonable _____ for their efforts?

6. If he would only devote more time in school to serious study and less to _____ pranks, his grades would probably improve.

7. It is one thing to offer a personal opinion; it is quite another to issue a(n) _____ as though you were the only one with any knowledge of the subject.

8. Since she thoroughly enjoys taking potshots at sacred cows, I'd describe her attitude as definitely _____ .

9. I was an extremely sensitive child, and the death of my beloved mother certainly had a(n) _____ effect upon me.

10. The speaker paid no attention to the _____ remarks of a few hecklers in the crowd but went right on with her speech.

11. In our bored and depressed mood, her buoyant personality had a most _____ effect.

12. Though the critic still has nothing good to say about modern art, age and experience have somewhat _____ the intensity of his disapproval.

13. The deathbed scene might have been effective if it had been played with taste and restraint, but their woefully ham-handed acting turned it into a(n) _____ tearjerker.

14. To gain the immediate attention of the reader, the short-story writer usually begins a narrative _____ , rather than at the very beginning of events.

15. If you are so _____ in handling your own personal affairs, how can you presume to advise others how to manage their lives?

16. All the evidence that has been offered at such length and at such costs to our patience does not seriously _____ the case against the accused.

17. A group of elderly people sitting about sipping tea and discussing the weather is scarcely my idea of _____ revelry.

18. I certainly have no intention of turning my back on them simply because it has been _____ about town that they are involved in some sort of scandal.

19. And such are the quirks of fate that there she was, after all her mishaps and blunders, firmly _____ as the president of the firm.

20. What we are facing in this organization is not "healthy competition" among the executives, but a(n) _____ struggle that will destroy the entire company if it is not halted.

Synonyms   *Choose the word for this unit that is most nearly **the same** in meaning as each of the following expressions. Write it in the space given.*

1. beneficial, healthy, invigorating   _____

2. to impair; to degrade; to undermine   _____

3. a maxim, precept, aphorism, axiom   _____

4. inept, awkward, clumsy; gauche   _____

5. a criterion, yardstick, benchmark   _____

6. foresight, foreknowledge   _____

7. whimsical, droll, jocular   _____

8. image-breaking, irreverent, heretical   _____

9. vituperative, scurrilous, excoriating   _____

10. to regulate, adjust, adapt, moderate   _____

11. to settle, to nestle, lodge, entrench   _____

12. murderous, savage, ruinous; intramural   _____

13. foreboding, ominous; pretentious   _____

14. miscarried, fruitless; premature   _____

15. to noise abroad, broadcast, blazon   _____

16. sentimental, mushy, mawkish   _____

17. shocking, jolting   _____

18. dissipated, debauched, orgiastic   _____

19. a swap, trade, one thing for another   _____

50

20. into the middle of things _____

Antonyms *Choose the word for this unit that is most nearly **opposite** in meaning to each of the following groups of expressions. Write it in the space given.*

1. successful, realized, consummated _____

2. sedate, prim, decorous, seemly _____

3. to purify; to fortify, strengthen; to enhance _____

4. auspicious, propitious, encouraging _____

5. skillful, dexterous, deft, tactful _____

6. hindsight _____

7. harmful, unhealthy, deleterious, noxious _____

8. serious, grave, grim, dour, humorless _____

9. to cover up, conceal; to hush up _____

10. peaceful, harmonious; constructive _____

11. soothing, comforting, agreeable, pleasant _____

12. laudatory, commendatory; deferential _____

13. orthodox, conservative, reverent _____

14. to unseat, displace, oust _____

Choosing the Right Word *Circle the **boldface** word that more satisfactorily completes each of the following sentences.*

1. A rugged sense of honesty, marked by a refusal to take refuge in clever ambiguities and facile verbalisms, has been the (**touchstone, dictum**) of my public career.

2. Some people seem to be natural nonconformists; for them (**prescience, iconoclasm**) is not just a mood or an affectation but a way of life.

3. With her elegance and remarkable feel for style, is it any wonder that she soon became (**vitiated, ensconced**) as the arbiter of fashion?

4. When the miners arrived with all their back pay and intent upon "having fun," our little town soon took on the aspect of a frontier (**saturnalia, dictum**).

5. All the snide rumors that have been spread about them do not (**vitiate, ensconce**) their solid reputation for authentic kindness and decency.

6

6. Historians believe that the Civil War left a sort of collective (**trauma, in media res**), which was not healed until a new generation had grown to maturity.

7. Willy-nilly, parents are often forced to enter (**in medias res, waggishly**) into a quarrel between siblings, especially when lasting damage seems about to occur.

8. Their efforts to settle the differences between the two factions were so (**portentous, maladroit**) that what had begun as a rift became a yawning chasm.

9. Prior to the Wright brothers' first successful airplane flight in 1903, all of mankind's efforts to fly had been (**internecine, abortive**).

10. The sharp decline in the value of the company's stock was attributed to the fact that rumors of the cancellation of the big contract had been (**bruited, vitiated**) about widely.

11. In that unhappy situation, I don't know which was more distressing—the callous indifference of some of my alleged "friends" or the (**maudlin, contumelious**) sympathy of others.

12. My plan to run in the primaries will not be diverted by the (**touchstone, dicta**) of so-called experts who assert that I have no chance of winning.

13. In spite of my extreme nervousness, I made every effort to (**modulate, bruit**) my voice and speak the first lines in a calm, controlled manner.

14. Of all the qualities that enabled them to survive during the critical years, the most vital was the uncanny (**prescience, dictum**) with which they anticipated the moves of their enemies.

15. Although those supposedly (**abortive, waggish**) remarks were dressed in the guise of humor, they betrayed a strong undertone of resentment.

16. Our hope for peace rests basically on the belief that the great powers now realize that warfare has become (**internecine, saturnalian**).

17. Even the most hardened campaigner might be expected to cringe when subjected to that kind of (**waggish, contumelious**) treatment.

18. I felt that I had stated my case with sincerity and conviction, but my heart sank when they reacted with a (**maladroit, portentous**) silence.

19. Their cool and detached skepticism, which I would have resented under other circumstances, now struck me as a (**portentous, salubrious**) factor in that highly emotionalized situation.

20. The concessions which we are making in this treaty are manifest, but I am unable to recognize a reasonable (**prescience, quid pro quo**) from the other side.

Review Units 4–6

Analogies   In each of the following, encircle the letter of the item that best completes the comparison.

1. touchstone is to **test** as
a. yardstick is to measure
b. scale is to estimate
c. gauge is to guide
d. criterion is to balance

2. maudlin is to **sentiment** as
a. piquant is to flour
b. unctuous is to acid
c. saccharine is to sugar
d. acerbic is to oil

3. ineffable is to **express** as
a. illegible is to write
b. incalculable is to compute
c. imponderable is to deny
d. inscrutable is to puzzle

4. prison is to **immure** as
a. hospital is to try
b. barn is to reform
c. school is to punish
d. cemetery is to inter

5. waggish is to **jester** as
a. mendacious is to liar
b. tendentious is to judge
c. contumelious is to diplomat
d. insouciant is to juggler

6. maladroit is to **skill** as
a. sage is to wisdom
b. erudite is to knowledge
c. prestigious is to celebrity
d. feckless is to will power

7. bilious is to **nauseate** as
a. disquieting is to elate
b. traumatic is to shock
c. benign is to alarm
d. portentous is to reassure

8. obsequies are to **die** as
a. nuptials are to wed
b. philippics are to graduate
c. dicta are to divorce
d. lucubrations are to age

9. aficionado is to **enthusiastic** as
a. persona is to personable
b. braggart is to demure
c. pundit is to knowledgeable
d. craven is to valiant

10. sacred cow is to **sacrosanct** as
a. paper tiger is to prurient
b. red herring is to misleading
c. white elephant is to salubrious
d. lame duck is to dexterous

Identifications   In each of the following groups, circle the word that is best defined or suggested by the introductory phrase.

1. Let me look into the crystal ball for you.
a. ensconce   b. divination   c. obsequies   d. genre

2. the deeds of Superman and Wonder Woman
a. browbeat   b. derring-do   c. homily   d. corollary

3. cold springwater after a six-mile summertime jog
a. touchstone   b. matrix   c. dictum   d. elixir

4. Spring, forward; fall, back.
a. parameter   b. cul-de-sac   c. folderol   d. mnemonic

5. a sudden about-face
a. volte-face   b. affinity   c. emolument   d. systemic

6. the ups and downs of life
a. maudlin   b. vitiate   c. vicissitudes   d. traumatic

7. Get as good as you give.
a. abortive   b. gamut   c. quid pro quo   d. prurient

8. You have to have style!
a. portentous   b. saturnalian   c. bilious   d. panache

9. how a bird in a gilded cage might feel
a. prescience   b. immured   c. symptomatic   d. aficionado

10. see-through curtains
a. ineffable   b. diaphanous   c. tendentious   d. risible

11. where the *Aeneid* starts
a. in medias res   b. sacrosanct   c. ensconce   d. pundit

12. How did you know that this would happen?
a. waggish   b. prescience   c. cognate   d. iconoclastic

13. how you might characterize a klutz
a. maladroit   b. obloquy   c. foray   d. lucubration

14. the endless bickering that is tearing apart a family
a. internecine   b. bruit   c. salubrious   d. contumelious

Shades of Meaning   *Read each sentence carefully. Then encircle the item that best completes the sentence below it.*

In some religions the name of the deity is considered ineffable, and believers forbear to utter it for fear of inviting divine retribution. **(2)**

1. In line 1 the word **ineffable** is used to mean
a. utterly inexpressible
b. too sacred to be spoken
c. absolutely indescribable
d. unknowable

Since the common cold is caused by a viral infection for which there is as yet no cure, medicine can do no more than offer a symptomatic treatment of the malady. **(2)**

2. The word **symptomatic** in line 2 most nearly means
a. characteristic
b. indicative
c. typically old-fashioned
d. relating to symptoms

When television was first introduced, most critics dismissed it as a folderol, never dreaming it would evolve into the ubiquitous and dominant arbiter of popular culture that it has since become. **(2)**

3. The best definition for the word **folderol** in line 1 is
a. trifle   b. gibberish   c. hoopla   d. innovation

They who ensconced the papyrus and leather documents now known as the Dead Sea Scrolls could scarcely have dreamed that nearly two thousand years would pass before the manuscripts they had hidden would see light of day once more. **(2)** **(4)**

4. In line 1 the word **ensconced** most nearly means
a. nestled   b. settled   c. entrenched   d. hid

"The Moor replies
That he you hurt is of great fame in Cyprus, **(2)**
and great affinity, and that in wholesome wisdom
He might not but refuse you."   (Shakespeare, *Othello,* III, 1, 43–46) **(4)**

5. The phrase [**of**] **great affinity** in line 3 is used to mean
a. widely connected
b. naturally inclined
c. much attracted
d. very powerful

54

Antonyms   *In each of the following groups, circle the word or expression that is most nearly **opposite** in meaning to the first word in **boldface** type.*

1. prurient
a. prudish
b. salacious
c. tiresome
d. polluted

2. bilious
a. delightful
b. peevish
c. punctual
d. impoverished

3. tendentious
a. peaceful
b. disinterested
c. argumentative
d. violent

4. affinity
a. conclusion
b. eternity
c. similarity
d. aversion

5. corollary
a. instrument
b. eve
c. axiom
d. malapropism

6. portentous
a. silly
b. dispassionate
c. auspicious
d. immature

7. risible
a. falling
b. slanderous
c. heartrending
d. indirect

8. obloquy
a. confusion
b. acclaim
c. vilification
d. clarify

9. contumelious
a. provocative
b. complimentary
c. disdainful
d. ample

10. maladroit
a. tactful
b. inquisitive
c. sturdy
d. floundering

11. immure
a. prepare
b. enclose
c. suffer
d. liberate

12. traumatic
a. dangerous
b. trustworthy
c. soothing
d. sage

13. cognate
a. unrelated
b. expensive
c. recent
d. weird

14. folderol
a. trifle
b. humor
c. sense
d. sentiment

15. iconoclastic
a. rational
b. conservative
c. decisive
d. aggressive

16. salubrious
a. tasty
b. hygienic
c. noxious
d. welcome

17. waggish
a. droll
b. humorless
c. shifty
d. inflexible

18. vitiate
a. enhance
b. destroy
c. create
d. debase

19. abortive
a. consummated
b. untimely
c. idealistic
d. reveling

20. insouciant
a. open
b. distraught
c. conditional
d. guarded

Completing the Sentence   *From the following groups of words, choose the one that best completes each of the sentences below. Write the word in the space provided.*

Group A

bruit	**vicissitude**	**emolument**	**in medias res**
aficionado	**modulate**	**cognate**	**elixir**

1. Though modern "alchemists" continue the age-old search for the putative _____ of life, I don't think any such nostrum exists.

2. A true _____ of baseball can reel off the batting average of every member of the Hall of Fame.

3. Unfortunately, the _____ of a college professor is almost always considerably lower than that of an executive in the business world.

4. Just growing up often _____ the intensity of our reactions to things we like or dislike.

5. You have no right to change the rules _____ just because you're losing!

Group B

vitiate	**tendentious**	**dictum**	**salubrious**
sacrosanct	**foray**	**affinity**	**derring-do**

1. That Errol Flynn movie on the Late Show was full of utterly incredible but delightful feats of _____ .

2. It was only too clear that the years of power, privilege, and good living had served to _____ his youthful idealism.

3. We believe in being courteous and considerate to one another, but we certainly don't regard every minor detail of etiquette and protocol as

_____ .

4. I can't get along with someone who is so _____ that any opinion I may express is taken as a pretext for a full-dress argument.

5. I know that you are a highly prestigious literary critic, but I refuse to accept passively every _____ you may issue on what is or is not worth reading.

Word Families

A. *On the line provided, write a **noun** related to each of the following words.*

EXAMPLE: bilious—**biliousness**

1. risible _____
2. ineffable _____
3. symptomatic _____
4. insouciant _____
5. prurient _____
6. systemic _____
7. abortive _____
8. contumelious _____
9. iconoclastic _____
10. portentous _____
11. saturnalian _____
12. traumatic _____

13. waggish _____

14. modulate _____

15. tendentious _____

B. *On the line provided, write a **verb** related to each of the following words.*

Example: divination—**divine**

1. portentous _____

2. dictum _____

3. systemic _____

4. abortive _____

5. traumatic _____

6. persona _____

Filling the Blanks *Encircle the pair of words that best complete the meaning of each of the following passages.*

1. Famous for his daring _____ deep behind Northern lines, J.E.B. Stuart, the South's most colorful cavalry commander, led his men on one dangerous mission after another with all the _____ and style of one of Charlemagne's legendary paladins.

  a. obsequies . . . persona   c. philippics . . . derring-do
  b. emoluments . . . prescience   d. forays . . . panache

2. When he realized that flattery was getting him nowhere, he attempted to _____ me into acquiescence, but, here again, his efforts proved _____ .

  a. bruit . . . risible   c. vitiate . . . tendentious
  b. browbeat . . . abortive   d. modulate . . . maladroit

3. In one of her more devastating _____ , Dorothy Parker is reputed to have once observed that an incompetent actor's interpretation of a role ran the _____ of emotions from A to B.

  a. dicta . . . gamut   c. corollaries . . . cul-de-sac
  b. lucubrations . . . mnemonic   d. homilies . . . parameters

4. Though I can't say that I relish the thriller as a literary form, I'm a real _____ of the detective _____ .

  a. pundit . . . touchstone   c. aficionado . . . genre
  b. iconoclast . . . matrix   d. persona . . . folderol

Analogies   *In each of the following, choose the item that best completes the comparison.*

1. waggish is to **laughs** as
a. risible is to yawns
b. bilious is to smiles
c. lachrymose is to tears
d. ribald is to sneers

2. diaphanous is to **veils** as
a. noisome is to clouds
b. gossamer is to cobwebs
c. bulky is to showers
d. abortive is to breezes

3. microcosm is to **macrocosm** as
a. plethora is to paucity
b. poltroon is to craven
c. purview is to orbit
d. parameter is to touchstone

4. homily is to **church** as
a. sermon is to air show
b. diatribe is to game show
c. aria is to horse show
d. monologue is to talk show

5. mnemonic is to **memory** as
a. trousers are to speech
b. glasses are to vision
c. earmuffs are to movement
d. blinders are to hearing

6. salubrious is to **health** as
a. pragmatic is to validity
b. eleemosynary is to profit
c. tendentious is to justice
d. therapeutic is to recovery

7. insouciant is to **concern** as
a. oblivious is to consciousness
b. sanguine is to optimism
c. quizzical is to erudition
d. portentous is to intrepidity

8. tearjerker is to **maudlin** as
a. opera is to prurient
b. tragedy is to risible
c. farce is to hilarious
d. satire is to heartrending

9. philippic is to **vituperative** as
a. liturgy is to ribald
b. encomium is to complimentary
c. harangue is to restrained
d. paean is to scurrilous

10. klutz is to **maladroit** as
a. bigot is to intolerant
b. dynamo is to supine
c. aficionado is to blasé
d. pundit is to ignorant

Shades of Meaning   *Read each sentence carefully. Then encircle the item that best completes the sentence below it.*

One of the great masters of genre painting is the Dutch artist Jan Vermeer, whose depictions of everyday scenes seem magically infused with light and life.   (2)

1. The word **genre** in line 1 most nearly means
a. still-life   b. realist   c. abstract   d. category

Herman Melville's masterpiece *Moby Dick* is prefaced by a sort of lexicon of etymological entries and quoted passages having to do with whales and whaling.   (2)

2. The best definition for the word **lexicon** in line 1 is
a. glossary   b. dictionary   c. wordbook   d. compendium

I will grant that manners and mores may change with the times, but common courtesy is never effete.   (2)

3. In line 2 the word **effete** is used to mean
a. exhausted   b. sterile   c. out of date   d. enfeebled

The toll taken on the cavalry by hunger and disease showed as much in
the hidebound mounts as in the hollow-eyed and drooping troopers
astride them. **(2)**

4. In line 2 the word **hidebound** is used to mean
a. narrow-minded   c. conservative
b. gaunt   d. rigid

"These late eclipses in the sun and moon portend no good to us. Though
the wisdom of nature can reason thus and thus, yet nature finds itself **(2)**
scourged by the sequent effects."
      (Shakespeare, *King Lear,* I, 2, 103–106)

5. The word **portend** in line 1 most nearly means
a. inspire awe   c. forebode
b. offer   d. conjure

Filling
the Blanks   *Encircle the pair of words that best complete each of*
     the following passages.

1. The _____ of the forty _____ contained in
Sketches of Country Life is truly extraordinary, and the reader is left with
the distinct impression that he or she actually knows the people who are
being described.
a. poltroonery . . . enclaves   c. rapacity . . . paeans
b. verisimilitude . . . vignettes   d. virtuosity . . . claques

2. Recently, many Christian denominations have modernized the language of
the _____ that they use in their services because it had
become clear that the presence of obsolete words and phrases in the
traditional material tended to _____ the meaning of the rites
for contemporary congregations.
a. homilies . . . bowdlerize   c. lucubrations . . . vitiate
b. obsequies . . . bruit   d. liturgies . . . obfuscate

3. In Gaetano Donizetti's famous comic opera *The* _____ *of*
Love, a clever charlatan _____ an overly gullible country
bumpkin into believing that a plain old bottle of Bordeaux wine is in fact a
powerful love potion that will solve the poor yokel's amorous problems
overnight.
a. *Mnemonic* . . . apprises   c. *Parameter* . . . browbeats
b. *Elixir* . . . cozens   d. *Vassal* . . . forays

4. Prudish Victorians were so offended by the _____ jokes and
salacious language in some of Shakespeare's plays that they would only
read his works in heavily _____ versions.
a. prurient . . . polarized   c. ribald . . . bowdlerized
b. risible . . . vitiated   d. ineffable . . . deracinated

Unit 7

Group A

abeyance	debauch
ambivalent	éclat
beleaguer	fastidious
carte blanche	gambol
cataclysm	imbue

Pronunciation Match each of the words contained in Group A with its phonetic transcription. Write the appropriate word in the space given.

1. 'kärt blänsh   _____

2. am 'biv ə lənt   _____

3. 'gam bəl   _____

4. bi 'lē gər   _____

5. di 'bôch   _____

6. im 'byü   _____

7. ə 'bā əns   _____

8. ā 'klä   _____

9. 'kat ə kliz əm   _____

10. fa 'stid ē əs   _____

Definition Choose the word from Group A that most nearly corresponds to each of the definitions below. Write the word in the blank space at the right of the definition and then in the illustrative phrase below it.

1. (*v.*) to jump or skip about playfully   _____

_____ like lambs in a meadow

2. (*adj.*) having opposite and conflicting feelings about someone or something   _____

a deeply _____ attitude toward the plan

3. (*n.*) dazzling or conspicuous success or acclaim; great brilliance (of performance or achievement)   _____

dazzled by the _____ of his performance

4. (*n.*) a state of being temporarily inactive, suspended, or set aside   _____

hold the matter in _____

5. (*v.*) to soak or stain thoroughly; to fill the mind   _____

_____ with the desire to succeed

6. (*n*.) full freedom or authority to act at one's own discretion   _____

gave us _____ in the matter

7. (*adj*.) overly demanding or hard to please; excessively careful in regard to details; easily disgusted   _____

noted for her _____ taste

8. (*n*.) a sudden, violent, or devastating upheaval; a surging flood, deluge   _____

the _____ of World War I

9. (*v*.) to set upon from all sides; to surround with an army; to trouble, harass   _____

_____ the fortress

10. (*v*.) to corrupt morally, seduce; to indulge in dissipation; (*n*.) an act or occasion of dissipation or vice   _____

those who would _____ the innocent

Group B

inchoate	**philistine**
lampoon	**picaresque**
malleable	**queasy**
nemesis	**refractory**
opt	**savoir-faire**

Pronunciation   *Match each of the words contained in Group B with its phonetic transcription. Write the appropriate word in the space given.*

1. ′fil i stēn *or* ′fil i stīn   _____

2. in ′kō it   _____

3. sav wär ′fâr   _____

4. ′kwē zē   _____

5. ′mal ē ə bəl   _____

6. lam ′pün   _____

7. ri ′frak tə rē   _____

8. pik ə ′resk   _____

9. opt   _____

10. ′nem ə sis   _____

7

Definition   *Choose the word from Group B that most nearly corresponds to each of the definitions listed below. Write the word in the blank space to the right of the definition and then in the illustrative phrase below it.*

1. (*n.*) a malicious satire; (*v.*) to satirize, ridicule   _____

   _____ the dictator

2. (*n.*) the ability to say and do the right thing in any situation; social competence   _____

   handled with surprising _____

3. (*adj.*) nauseated or uneasy; causing nausea or uneasiness; troubled   _____

   a(n) _____ feeling in the pit of my stomach

4. (*adj.*) just beginning; not fully shaped or formed   _____

   a molten and _____ mass

5. (*adj.*) involving or characteristic of clever rogues or adventurers   _____

   the _____ element in the novel

6. (*v.*) to make a choice or decision   _____

   finally _____ for the cheaper model

7. (*adj.*) stubborn; hard or difficult to manage; not responsive to treatment or cure   _____

   a(n) _____ child

8. (*adj.*) lacking in, hostile to, or smugly indifferent to cultural and artistic values or refinements; (*n.*) such a person   _____

   a _____ contempt for art

9. (*n.*) an agent or force inflicting vengeance or punishment; retribution itself; an unbeatable rival   _____

   proved to be my _____

10. (*adj.*) capable of being formed into different shapes; capable of being altered, adapted, or influenced   _____

    the _____ minds of the young

Completing the Sentence   *Choose the word for this unit that best completes each of the following sentences. Write it in the space given.*

1. There are circumstances under which it is desirable to make decisions swiftly and unequivocally, but there are other cases in which it is wise to

   hold decisions in _____ .

2. I was confident that I would do well in the scholarship examination, but my hopes were dashed by my old _____ , mathematics.

3. As we turned into the ranch, we saw two young colts _____ playfully in the open field.

4. Oscar's careless housekeeping and sloppy habits were an endless source of exasperation to his _____ roommate.

5. The purpose of the course in American history is to _____ young people with a genuine understanding and appreciation of what this country stands for.

6. You made some rather clever suggestions at the meeting, but on the whole your ideas were far too _____ to serve as the basis for a workable plan.

7. They showed such a deplorable lack of _____ in handling that difficult situation that they converted a mere unpleasantness into a social disaster.

8. Perhaps once in a generation, a people is faced with a great moral crisis in which it must _____ for good or evil, war or peace, life or death.

9. Since I had unlimited faith in their honestly and discretion, I felt no qualms about giving them _____ to do whatever they thought was necessary.

10. The young pianist dazzled the audience with the _____ and verve of his performance.

11. Many scientists are fearful that the West Coast may someday suffer a(n) _____ as violent as the earthquake that devastated San Francisco in 1906.

12. Her equivocal answers to my questions about going to college in the fall clearly revealed her _____ attitude toward leaving home.

13. Should we expect the needs and purposes of a true poet to be understood by such a thoroughgoing _____ ?

14. The entire issue of the magazine was designed as a(n) _____ satirizing the follies and futilities of mass-consumption advertising.

15. Though Jane's mount was as docile as a newborn lamb, mine proved to be the most _____ animal I had ever ridden.

16. I freely confess that just the sight of a roller coaster is enough to make me feel _____ .

7

17. Instead of settling down to a job and a family, Tom seems to be modeling his life on the career of some rogue out of a(n) _____ novel.

18. Such capacity for growth and self-improvement can be expected only in the _____ years of the teens and early twenties.

19. A host of creditors _____ the hapless businessman with demands for payment and threats of legal action.

20. How could they have _____ themselves by joining in that obscene celebration?

Synonyms   *Choose the word for this unit that is most nearly the* ***same*** *in meaning as each of the following groups of expressions. Write it in the space provided.*

1. pliable, impressionable, adaptable   _____

2. incipient, embryonic, rudimentary   _____

3. to frolic, romp, cavort, caper   _____

4. deferment, postponement, suspension   _____

5. to corrupt, seduce, carouse; a spree, orgy   _____

6. to infuse, instill, inculcate   _____

7. a disaster, catastrophe, upheaval   _____

8. roguish, rascally, rakish   _____

9. tact, finesse, suavity, sophistication   _____

10. to satirize, parody, ridicule; a burlesque   _____

11. a blank check, free rein   _____

12. to besiege, encircle; to harass, pester   _____

13. nauseous, uneasy, troubled, unsettled   _____

14. acclaim, celebrity; brilliance   _____

15. to choose, select, decide   _____

16. unruly, disobedient; willful, mulish   _____

17. retribution, comeuppance; an avenger   _____

18. precise, meticulous, exacting, finicky   _____

19. equivocal, ambiguous, of two minds   _____

20. boorish, lowbrow; a yahoo   _____

Antonyms   *Choose the word for this unit that is most nearly **opposite** in meaning to each of the following groups of expressions. Write it in the space given.*

1. refined, cultivated; an esthete, highbrow   _____

2. rigid, inflexible, unyielding, intractable   _____

3. a guardian angel, ally, patron   _____

4. careless, sloppy, messy, untidy, slovenly   _____

5. docile, tractable, dutiful, obedient   _____

6. mature, developed, complete   _____

7. tactlessness, gaucherie, boorishness   _____

8. to elevate, uplift, inspire; to purify   _____

9. unequivocal, unambigious, clear-cut   _____

10. to remove, expunge, eradicate, erase   _____

11. calm, untroubled, confident   _____

12. a compliment, flattery, homage   _____

13. dullness, insipidity, mediocrity   _____

14. to lumber, trudge, plod, drag one's feet   _____

Choosing the   *Circle the **boldface** word that more satisfactorily*
Right Word   *completes each of the following sentences.*

1. Perhaps you hope to divert our attention from your own misconduct by maliciously (**lampooning, gamboling**) a sincere and able public official.

2. Although we disagreed with much that you said, we could not help admiring the rhetorical brilliance and (**cataclysm, éclat**) of your writing style.

3. Their obsession with military conquest, leading them to waste their vast resources on armaments and endless wars, proved to be their (**nemesis, gambol**).

4. Refusing to become flustered, she handled the embarrassing situation with the finesse and (**queasiness, savoir-faire**) of a born diplomat.

5. Their (**fastidious, ambivalent**) preoccupation with minor details of style is not to be confused with a genuine feeling for language.

6. Would it not be a gross miscarriage of justice to prosecute us under a law which, for all practical purposes, has been in (**abeyance, carte blanche**) since the early years of this century?

7

7. With plenty of free time and with an excellent library at my disposal, I gave myself up to a delightful (**cataclysm, debauch**) of reading.

8. Instead of endless lamentations about how bad things are, let us try to look realistically at the (**lampoons, options**) open to us.

9. In the last analysis all lines of authority and responsibility lead back to the President; he cannot give (**carte blanche, nemesis**) to any assistant.

10. She was completely bewildered by the exhibition of abstract art, but, fearing to be labeled a (**lampoon, philistine**), she pretended to understand what she was looking at.

11. James Thurber's stories are extremely funny, but they are also (**imbued, debauched**) with a profound sense of the pathos of the human condition.

12. Because Thurber combines humor and pathos so masterfully, we might say that the mood of his stories is (**malleable, ambivalent**).

13. With all the misplaced confidence of inexperienced youth, I set out to make a million dollars by (**gamboling, imbuing**) in the not-so-verdant pastures of Wall Street.

14. He will never realize his full athletic potential as long as he remains (**beleaguered, opted**) by doubts about his own ability.

15. Although his poetry is somewhat crude and (**inchoate, fastidious**), it has a primitive energy and drive that many readers find extremely attractive.

16. It is one thing to be open-minded and (**queasy, malleable**); it is quite another to be without fixed ideas or principles of any kind.

17. Perhaps she felt disturbed at the prospect of having to betray her friends, but she seems to have overcome her (**queasiness, éclat**) without too much trouble.

18. In spite of his courage and love of adventure, he lacks the stature of a true hero; his character might better be described as (**picaresque, abeyant**).

19. Since they had always been reasonably well-behaved, I was utterly taken aback by their (**ambivalent, refractory**) behavior.

20. Another world war would be a(n) (**éclat, cataclysm**) on so vast a scale that it is doubtful whether civilization could survive it.

Unit 8

Group A

aberration	casuistry
ad hoc	de facto
bane	depredation
bathos	empathy
cantankerous	harbinger

Pronunciation *Match each of the words contained in Group A with its phonetic transcription. Write it in the space given.*

1. bān _____

2. 'ad 'häk _____

3. 'här bən jər _____

4. 'em pə thē _____

5. kan 'taŋ kə rəs _____

6. ab ə 'rā shən _____

7. 'bā thos _____

8. 'kazh ū is trē _____

9. dep rə 'da shən _____

10. dē 'fak tō _____

Definition *Choose the word from Group A that most nearly corresponds to each of the definitions below. Write the word in the blank space at the right of the definition and then in the illustrative phrase below it.*

1. (*adj.*) for this specific purpose; improvised; (*adv.*) with respect to this   _____

a(n) _____ committee

2. (*n.*) the act of preying upon or plundering   _____

the _____ of the invaders

3. (*n.*) a forerunner, herald; (*v.*) to herald the approach of   _____

a(n) _____ of spring

4. (*adj.*) actually existing or in effect, although not legally required or sanctioned; (*adv.*) in reality, actually   _____

the _____ head of state

5. (*n.*) a departure from what is proper, right, expected, or normal; a lapse from a sound metal state   _____

a(n) _____ of judgment

6. (*n.*) a sympathetic understanding of or identification with the feelings, thoughts, or attitudes of someone or something else

    felt _____ for their aspirations

7. (*n.*) the intrusion of commonplace or trite material into a context whose tone is lofty or elevated; grossly insincere or exaggerated sentimentality; the lowest phase, nadir; an anticlimax, comedown

    wallowing in _____

8. (*n.*) the source or cause of fatal injury, death, destruction, or ruin; death or ruin itself; poison

    rain, the _____ of picnics

9. (*adj.*) ill-tempered, quarrelsome; difficult to get along or deal with

    a(n) _____ machine

10. (*n.*) the determination of right and wrong in questions of conduct or conscience by the application of general ethical principles; specious argument

    nothing more than ingenious _____

Group B

hedonism	pander
lackluster	peccadillo
malcontent	pièce de résistance
mellifluous	remand
nepotism	syndrome

Pronunciation   *Match each of the words contained in Group B with its phonetic transcription. Write it in the space given.*

1. ′sin drōm _____

2. pek ə ′dil ō _____

3. ′pan dər _____

4. ′hē də niz əm _____

5. pē əs də rā zē ′stäns _____

6. ′nep ə tiz əm _____

7. ′lak lus tər _____

8. ri ′mand _____

9. mə ′lif lü əs _____

10. ′mal kən tent _____

68

Definition Choose the word from Group B that most nearly corresponds to each of the following definitions. Write the word in the blank space at the right of the definition and then in the illustrative phrase below it.

1. (*n.*) a minor sin or offense; a trifling fault or shortcoming _____

overlook my _____

2. (*n.*) a group of symptoms or signs that collectively characterize or indicate a disease, disorder, abnormality, etc. _____

a decidedly modern _____

3. (*n.*) undue favoritism to or excessive patronage of one's relatives _____

avoid any taint of _____

4. (*n.*) the belief that the attainment of pleasure is life's chief aim; devotion to or pursuit of pleasure _____

the beach bum's mindless _____

5. (*n.*) The principal dish of a meal; the principal event, incident, or item; an outstanding accomplishment _____

the _____ of that remarkable repast

6. (*v.*) to send or order back; in law, to send back to jail or to a lower court _____

was _____ to the custody of the sheriff

7. (*v.*) to cater to or provide satisfaction for the low tastes or vices of others; (*n.*) a person who does this _____

_____ to their every whim

8. (*adj.*) flowing sweetly or smoothly; honeyed _____

a(n) _____ voice

9. (*adj.*) lacking brilliance or vitality; dull _____

a(n) _____ stare

10. (*adj.*) discontented with or in open defiance of prevailing conditions; (*n.*) such a person _____

a group of vocal _____

Completing the Sentence Choose the word for this unit that best completes each of the following sentences. Write it in the space given.

1. I think you are showing poor judgment in condemning them so severely for what is, after all, little more than a(n) _____ .

2. A high temperature, yellowish complexion, and general feeling of fatigue are all characteristic of the mononucleosis _____ .

3. Those sentimentalized effusions introduced a note of _____ into what should have been an occasion marked by dignity and restraint.

4. Yes, I believe in helping out relatives, but I haven't spent a lifetime building this business to make it a monument to _____ .

5. It took years for that country to recover from the _____ wrought by the Second World War and its concomitant social and economic dislocations.

6. It was hard to believe that the eager, vibrant youth I had known was now this shabby derelict, staring into space with _____ eyes.

7. Is it too optimistic to hope that your willingness to undertake that thankless task is the _____ of a new maturity and a more responsible attitude?

8. Would it be ungracious of me to suggest that the _____ of the feast, given on the menu as "filet mignon," had the taste and texture of old shoe leather?

9. The history of Nazi Germany and Fascist Italy teaches us that we should never let ourselves be blinded by the meretricious _____ of a demagogue, no matter how appealing it may appear at first glance.

10. How is one to explain that strange _____ from the habits and standards which he had followed for so many years?

11. Since they have followed a policy of bringing in executives and supervisors from the outside, instead of promoting from within their own ranks, the office is filled with grumbling _____ .

12. I find myself in the position of a(n) _____ supervisor; now I would like to have the title, salary, and privileges that go along with the job.

13. Like everyone else, I was charmed by the _____ tones of the speaker, but afterwards I could extract very little real meaning from what she said.

14. Those cases that call for further attention will be _____ to the proper agencies.

15. Yes, you have scored a quick commercial success, but you have done it only by _____ to low and depraved tastes.

16. The pitcher's lightning fastball has proved the _____ of many a celebrated home-run hitter.

17. Though he had embraced a creed of unabashed _____ in his youth, he ended his life among a group of ascetics living in the desert.

18. Since there was no agency concerned with race relations, the Mayor created a(n) _____ committee to deal with such matters.

19. He had been happy-go-lucky as a young man, but years of disappointment and misfortune have turned him sour and _____ .

20. Her visits to the nursing home are motivated not by a detached sense of duty but by a genuine _____ for those who are lonely.

Synonyms   *Choose the word for this unit that is most nearly the **same** as each of the following groups of expressions. Write it in the space given.*

1. cranky, testy, peevish, irascible, ornery   _____

2. existing, in actuality, in point of fact   _____

3. a herald, precursor; to presage   _____

4. dissatisfied, disgruntled; a grumbler   _____

5. dull, vapid, insipid, drab, flat   _____

6. destruction, ruin; a spoiler, bête noire   _____

7. sophistry, quibbling   _____

8. looting, plunder, pillage; an outrage   _____

9. mawkishness, mush, schmaltz   _____

10. a deviation, anomaly, irregularity   _____

11. the main dish, centerpiece, chef d'oeuvre   _____

12. a petty offense, indiscretion   _____

13. to remit, send back, return   _____

14. euphonious, honeyed, musical   _____

15. a pimp, procurer; to cater, indulge   _____

16. favoritism to relatives   _____

17. improvised, makeshift   _____

18. sympathy, compassion, identification   _____

19. pleasure-seeking, sensuality, sybaritism   _____

20. a complex, pattern, or group of symptoms   _____

8

Antonyms   *Choose the word for this unit that is most nearly the **opposite** of each of the following groups of expressions. Write it in the space given.*

1. a blessing, comfort, solace, balm   _____

2. satisfied, contented, complacent, smug   _____

3. shrill, strident, harsh, grating   _____

4. brilliant, radiant, dazzling   _____

5. de jure, by right   _____

6. insensitivity, callousness, detachment   _____

7. asceticism, puritanism, self-denial   _____

8. an aftermath, epilogue, sequel   _____

9. to forward to, send on; to release   _____

10. permanent, long-standing   _____

11. good-natured, sweet-tempered, genial   _____

12. a preliminary, hors d'oeuvre   _____

13. a felony, mortal sin, enormity, atrocity   _____

Choosing the Right Word   *Circle the **boldface** word that more satisfactorily completes each of the following sentences.*

1. So strong is my (**empathy, casuistry**) with the poems of Robert Frost that I often feel as though I could have written them myself.

2. In many respects it is a good movie, but, sadly, the director has allowed sentiment to spill over into sentimentality, and sentimentality into (**bathos, casuistry**).

3. The (**aberrations, depredations**) of the terrible disease could be seen only too clearly in her extreme emaciation and feebleness.

4. Although the law forbids residential separation of the races, we all know that a state of (**de facto, ad hoc**) segregation exists in some communities.

5. In all aspects of their behavior, they showed the self-indulgence, the absorption in their own concerns, the gross indifference to others that is characteristic of the true (**malcontent, hedonist**).

6. The negotiators agreed not to try to draw up an overall treaty but to deal with each specific problem on a(n) (**de facto, ad hoc**) basis.

7. The (**syndrome, bathos**) of poverty, drug addiction, and crime that afflicts our cities calls for remedial action on a truly national scale.

8. Then came Miss Bolton's cornet solo, which we all recognized immediately as the (**pièce de résistance, casuistry**) of that long musical evening.

9. How can you compare a mere social (**peccadillo, depredation**) with a misdeed that has caused such great harm to other people?

10. We must not assume that their behavior, however (**aberrant, mellifluous**) by conventional standards, is a sign of mental illness.

11. Your efforts to prove that because "no one is perfect," all moral standards are relative and therefore meaningless, struck me as sheer (**casuistry, hedonism**).

12. A candidate for high public office should seek to debate the issues on an objective level, instead of (**remanding, pandering**) to the prejudices and misconceptions of the times.

13. We may find (**malcontents, hedonists**) annoying, but the fact is that they often serve as "gadflies" to bring about desirable changes.

14. The car was forever breaking down or refusing to start, but its owner seemed to derive a sort of perverse satisfaction out of battling with the (**mellifluous, cantankerous**) old heap.

15. Said Churchill to the British people after the Munich agreement: "We must reject these (**mellifluous, malcontent**) assurance of 'peace in our time' and realize that we have sustained a crushing defeat."

16. True, we won the game, but I think our team gave a rather (**lackluster, malcontent**) performance in beating a weak opponent by so narrow a margin.

17. We learned with dismay that our application had been neither approved nor rejected, but (**pandered, remanded**) to a "higher authority for further consideration."

18. The (**baneful, mellifluous**) looks which they directed at us made it only too clear that we had little hope for mercy at their hands.

19. With the extreme cold and the deep snows still holding on, the gradual lengthening of the days was the only (**aberration, harbinger**) of spring.

20. "Am I to be accused of (**casuistry, nepotism**)," queried the Mayor, "just because my wife, daughter, brother, nephew, and maiden aunt happen to be the best applicants for those jobs?"

Unit 9

Group A

beatitude	fervid
bête noire	fetid
bode	gargantuan
dank	heyday
ecumenical	incubus

Pronunciation *Match each of the words contained in Group A with its phonetic transcription. Write the appropriate word in the space given.*

1. 'fər vid　　　　　　　　　　_____

2. bet 'nwär　　　　　　　　　_____

3. 'fet id　　　　　　　　　　 _____

4. 'iŋ kyə bəs　　　　　　　　_____

5. daŋk　　　　　　　　　　　_____

6. gär 'gan chū ən　　　　　　_____

7. bē 'at ə tüd　　　　　　　　_____

8. ek yü 'men i kəl　　　　　 _____

9. bōd　　　　　　　　　　　 _____

10. 'hā dā　　　　　　　　　　_____

Definition *Choose the word from Group A that most nearly corresponds to each of the following definitions. Write the appropriate word in the blank space at the right of the definition and then in the illustrative phrase below it.*

1. (*v.*) to be an omen of; to indicate by signs　　_____

　　　a smile that _____ good news

2. (*adj.*) having an unpleasant or offensive odor　　_____

　　　the stale, _____ air of the windowless room

3. (*n.*) a demon or evil spirit supposed to haunt human beings in their bedrooms at night; anything that oppresses or weighs upon one, like a nightmare　　_____

　　　a terrifying _____

4. (*n.*) the period of greatest power, vigor, success, or influence; the prime years　　_____

　　　the _____ of the clipper ship

5. (*adj.*) burning with enthusiasm or zeal; extremely heated

_____

_____ words of praise

6. (*adj.*) unpleasantly damp or wet

_____

the _____ atmosphere of a cave

7. (*n.*) a state of perfect happiness or blessedness; a blessing

_____

"the consummate _____ of wealth" (Ruskin)

8. (*adj.*) worldwide or universal in influence or application

_____

a(n) _____ council

9. (*n.*) someone or something that one especially dislikes, dreads, or avoids

_____

spinach, my old _____

10. (*adj.*) of immense size, volume, or capacity; enormous, prodigious

_____

a(n) _____ thirst for life

Group B

infrastructure	**protégé**
inveigle	**prototype**
kudos	**sycophant**
lagniappe	**tautology**
prolix	**truckle**

Pronunciation   *Match each of the words contained in Group B with its phonetic transcription. Write the appropriate word in the space given.*

1. ˈprō tə zhā _____

2. ˈtruk əl _____

3. ˈlan yap _____

4. tô ˈtol ə jē _____

5. in ˈvā gəl _____

6. ˈprō tə tīp _____

7. ˈkü dos _____

8. ˈsik ə fənt _____

9. prō ˈlix _____

10. ˈin frə strək chər _____

Definition *Choose the word from Group B that most nearly corresponds to each of the following definitions. Write the word in the space at the right of the definition and then in the illustrative phrase below it.*

1. (*v.*) to yield or submit tamely or submissively _____

would _____ to no one

2. (*n.*) needless repetition of an idea by using different but equivalent words; a redundancy _____

full of _____ and solecisms

3. (*n.*) a basic foundation or framework; a system of public works; the resources and facilities required for an activity; permanent military installations _____

the city's aging _____

4. (*adj.*) long-winded and wordy; tending to speak or write in such a way _____

a(n) _____ account of the wedding

5. (*n.*) an extra or unexpected gift or gratuity _____

a(n) _____ for a regular customer

6. (*n.*) someone who attempts to win favors or advance him- or herself by flattery or servile behavior; a slanderer, defamer _____

a two-faced _____

7. (*n.*) someone whose welfare, training, or career is under the patronage of an influential person; someone under the jurisdiction of a foreign country or government _____

the _____ of the ex-champion

8. (*n.*) the acclaim, prestige, or renown that comes as the result of some action or achievement _____

all the _____ due a Nobel laureate

9. (*n.*) an original pattern or model; a primitive or ancestral form _____

the _____ of the modern detective novel

10. (*v.*) to entice, lure, or snare by flattery or artful inducements; to obtain or acquire by artifice _____

eventually _____ us into joining them

Completing the Sentence *Choose the word that best completes each of the following sentences. Write it in the space given.*

1. I was happy enough when she agreed to go to the prom with me, but her

suggestion that we use her car was an unexpected _____ .

2. To maintain that because human beings are aggressive animals, they will always be involved in conflict with other members of their species seems to me a mere _____ .

3. Far better to receive sincere criticism, no matter how severe, than the groveling adulation of a(n) _____ .

4. As the _____ of one of the great violinists of our times, she has had an unrivaled opportunity to develop her musical talents.

5. I consider the vogue use of "hopefully" illogical, inept, and pretentious; it has become my linguistic _____ .

6. In *David Copperfield*, Dickens described with heartbreaking realism the period of his own childhood that he spent working as an apprentice in a(n) _____ and chilly cellar.

7. It was a subject of heated debate in the early 19th century whether the federal government should play any part at all in building the _____ to support the fledgling American economy.

8. The memory of my ghastly blunder and of the harm it had done to innocent people weighed on my spirit like a(n) _____ .

9. The atmosphere of distrust and hostility did not _____ well for the outcome of the peace talks.

10. The lame-duck President looked back with nostalgia on the power he had wielded during the _____ of his administration.

11. The speaker emphasized that in the modern world the barriers between different groups are rapidly being broken down and that we must try to think in truly _____ terms.

12. In H.G. Wells's *The Time Machine,* we see the _____ of a vast number of stories and novels in the area of science fiction.

13. Was it just our imagination, or was the room still _____ with the smell of stale cigar smoke?

14. I think it was terribly naive of us to expect to get a fair hearing from such _____ partisans of the opposing party.

15. In the dreamy _____ of their first love, nothing I might have said would have had the slightest effect on them.

16. After I read one of your _____ and repetitive reports, I always have the feeling that you are suffering from a terminal case of what might be called "diarrhea of the mouth."

17. At the risk of losing the election, I refused to _____ to the fleeting passions and prejudices of a small part of the electorate.

18. Falstaff is a behemoth of a man, whose _____ appetites, especially for sack and sleep, never seem to be satiated.

19. May I say in all modesty that I don't deserve such _____ just because I was all-state in football and basketball, led my class academically, and edited the school paper.

20. Like most people, I enjoy flattery, but I can't be _____ into doing something that in my heart I know is wrong.

Synonyms   *Choose the word for this unit that is most nearly the **same** in meaning as each of the following groups of expressions. Write it in the space given.*

1. long-winded, verbose, garrulous   _____

2. glory, praise, acclaim, accolades   _____

3. bliss, rapture; blessedness   _____

4. smelly, putrid, noisome, foul, malodorous   _____

5. a redundancy, repetition, pleonasm   _____

6. to kowtow, stoop, grovel; to yield   _____

7. an archetype, model, pattern, original   _____

8. clammy, moist, soggy, damp   _____

9. foundation, base, basis, underpinning   _____

10. huge, colossal, mammoth, gigantic   _____

11. to induce, beguile, cajole, wheedle   _____

12. a yes-man, toady, flunky, bootlicker   _____

13. worldwide, general, comprehensive   _____

14. a gratuity, bonus; the "icing on the cake"   _____

15. to presage, augur, foreshadow   _____

16. ardent, zealous, fervent, earnest   _____

17. the prime, "golden age"   _____

18. a demon, hobgoblin; a millstone, burden   _____

19. a pet peeve, bugbear, nemesis   _____

20. a ward, charge, disciple, trainee   _____

Antonyms　　*Choose the word for this unit that is most nearly* **opposite** *in meaning to each of the following groups of expressions. Write it in the space given.*

1. tiny, minuscule, infinitesimal, dwarfish _____

2. dry, arid, parched, desiccated _____

3. terse, laconic, succinct, pithy _____

4. to resist, defy, stand up to _____

5. apathetic, indifferent, cool, blasé _____

6. the formative years; the twilight years, decline _____

7. misery, despair _____

8. boos, disapproval, condemnation _____

9. fragrant, aromatic, perfumed, sweet _____

10. parochial, regional, insular _____

11. a pet, idol, apple of one's eye _____

12. superstructure _____

13. a copy, imitation _____

14. a sponsor, mentor, benefactor _____

Choosing the Right Word　　*Circle the* **boldface** *word that more satisfactorily completes each of the following sentences.*

1. I felt that I could not continue to live any longer in that (**dank, gargantuan**) atmosphere of prejudice and hostility.

2. When I saw the beautiful girl you had brought to the prom, I understood the reason for your smile of (**fetid, beatific**) self-satisfaction.

3. Her composition was seriously weakened by (**tautologies, beatitudes**) such as "an older woman who is approaching the end of her life span."

4. In the perspective of history, we can recognize that many customs and institutions that seemed, at a particular time, to be in their (**incubus, heyday**) were actually already on the decline.

5. In all the great religions, we find common ideals and standards that must be regarded as (**abrasive, ecumenical**) values, equally valid at all times and in all places.

6. Surrounded from earliest childhood by flattering courtiers, the monarch grew to adulthood unable to distinguish a friend from a (**lagniappe, sycophant**).

7. I had expected to be paid generously for my work, but the dazzling smile and gracious words with which she gave me the money were a delightful (**lagniappe, incubus**).

8. Surely you can make an honest effort to please your employer without incurring the charge that you are (**boding, truckling**) to the vanity of the person who pays your salary.

9. His zest for life and his boundless optimism were expressed perfectly, it seemed to me, in his (**gargantuan, fetid**) laughter.

10. My criticism of his statement is not merely that it is (**prolix, ecumenical**), but that it uses words to obscure rather than to sharpen and reinforce the meaning.

11. She became such a(n) (**abrasive, fervid**) supporter of the Los Angeles Dodgers that during the baseball season she seemed unable to speak of anything else.

12. When the sanitation strike continued into a second week, people began to complain about the (**fetid, fervid**) smell that hung over the sweltering city.

13. We didn't need a meteorologist to tell us that the lowering clouds and mounting winds did not (**bode, truckle**) well for our hopes for perfect beach weather.

14. Only then, in the twilight of her long career, did she begin to receive the (**heyday, kudos**) that her brilliant but unconventional writings so richly deserved.

15. I have no desire to be known as a nonconformist, but I am not going to allow fear of public disapproval to become my (**beatitude, bête noire**).

16. Scientists have for some time been correlating the functions of human consciousness with the neural (**tautology, infrastructure**) of the brain.

17. Our goal as a nation and as a society must be to free ourselves completely of the (**prototype, incubus**) of racial prejudice.

18. More than 400 years after his death, Leonardo da Vinci still stands out as the (**prototype, lagniappe**) of the universal genius, equally accomplished in science and in the arts.

19. You did nothing to help me during those difficult years, but now that I have achieved some success, you have the gall to claim me as your (**protégé, bête noire**).

20. Her story is that he wooed her relentlessly until she accepted his proposal; his story is that she (**truckled, inveigled**) him into marrying her.

Analogies   *In each of the following, choose the item that best completes the comparison.*

1. malleable is to **mold** as
a. ductile is to draw
b. senile is to compress
c. tensile is to shape
d. tactile is to melt

2. nemesis is to **retribution** as
a. incubus is to relief
b. bête noire is to satisfaction
c. harbinger is to death
d. bane is to ruin

3. curmudgeon is to **cantankerous** as
a. protégé is to intractable
b. philistine is to discriminating
c. sycophant is to obsequious
d. nepotist is to impartial

4. mellifluous is to **honey** as
a. unctuous is to vinegar
b. vitriolic is to acid
c. piquant is to oil
d. acerbic is to sugar

5. inveigle is to **blandishments** as
a. coerce is to compliments
b. wheedle is to reprimands
c. intimidate is to threats
d. cajole is to rebukes

6. hedonist is to **pleasure** as
a. atheist is to honor
b. vegetarian is to meat
c. materialist is to possessions
d. misanthrope is to friends

7. malcontent is to **disgruntled** as
a. virtuoso is to lackluster
b. fanatic is to fervid
c. pygmy is to gargantuan
d. slob is to fastidious

8. highway is to **infrastructure** as
a. embargo is to trade
b. icon is to culture
c. filibuster is to legislature
d. consumer is to economy

9. incubus is to **oppress** as
a. pet peeve is to nettle
b. bugbear is to amuse
c. pander is to edify
d. bête noire is to delight

10. satirist is to **lampoon** as
a. champion is to attack
b. eulogist is to extol
c. buttress is to undermine
d. critic is to defraud

Identification   *In each of the following groups, circle the word that is best defined or suggested by the introductory phrase.*

1. a complimentary calendar from the bank
a. incubus   b. lagniappe   c. ad hoc   d. nepotism

2. a crocus in early March
a. cantankerous   b. philistine   c. harbinger   d. casuistry

3. You'll be the death of me yet!
a. protégé   b. nemesis   c. syndrome   d. empathy

4. a behemoth of a man
a. gargantuan   b. bathos   c. lampoon   d. incubus

5. keep on ice for a time
a. beatitude   b. prototype   c. éclat   d. abeyance

6. The sight turned my stomach!
a. picaresque   b. malcontent   c. queasy   d. heyday

7. unequivocally and with all my heart
a. fetid   b. fervid   c. gargantuan   d. ecumenical

8. It just makes me see red!
a. beleaguer   b. truckle   c. kudos   d. bête noire

9. The highly touted Broadway play was less than exciting.
a. prolix   b. lackluster   c. depredation   d. remand

10. how you might characterize the First World War
a. savoir-faire   b. de facto   c. cataclysm   d. carte blanche

11. Don't try to sweet talk me!
a. lampoon   b. bode   c. tautology   d. inveigle

12. They never think of anything but their own enjoyment.
a. hedonism   b. bathos   c. bane   d. aberration

13. I'm of two minds about the idea.
a. abrasive   b. inchoate   c. ambivalent   d. dank

14. something you shouldn't make a federal case of
a. debauch   b. gambol   c. mellifluous   d. peccadillo

Shades of Meaning   *Read each sentence carefully. Then encircle the item that best completes the sentence below it.*

In December of 1776, when American fortunes were at bathos, George Washington rallied army morale and restored hope in the patriot cause with the daring crossing of the Delaware and the attack on Trenton.   **(2)**

1. In line 1 the word **bathos** most nearly means
a. mush   b. peak   c. sentimentality d. bottom

Medical authorities grew alarmed when the strange ailment proved refractory and, fearing an outbreak or even an epidemic, quarantined the stricken patients.   **(2)**

2. The best definition for the word **refractory** in line 2 is
a. untreatable   b. unruly   c. disobedient   d. stubborn

"Our natures do pursue,
Like rats that raven down their proper bane,   **(2)**
A thirsty evil; and when we drink, we die."
(Shakespeare, *Measure for Measure,* I, 2, 120–122)

3. The word **bane** in line 2 is used to mean
a. ruin   b. poison   c. death   d. destruction

"Given the ghoulish zeal with which the director inflicts these scenes of mayhem and carnage on the audience," observed the critic, "this is most definitely *not* a movie recommended for the fastidious."   **(2)**

4. In line 3 the word **fastidious** most nearly means
a. meticulous   c. easily disgusted
b. finicky   d. overly demanding

Because the accused was a protégé and therefore could not be tried, Federal prosecutors arranged to have him deported to his native land, there to be charged by his own government.   **(2)**

5. The word **protégé** in line 1 is used to mean
a. trainee   c. disciple
b. someone enjoying the patronage of a powerful person   d. someone under the protection of another government

Antonyms *In each of the following groups, circle the item that is most nearly **opposite** in meaning to the word in **boldface type**.*

1. éclat
a. abomination
b. curiosity
c. dullness
d. rarity

2. lackluster
a. distorted
b. dazzling
c. crass
d. beneficial

3. gambol
a. wager
b. trace
c. condemn
d. trudge

4. imbue
a. expunge
b. lend
c. infuse
d. cancel

5. fastidious
a. squeamish
b. cautious
c. slovenly
d. partial

6. fervid
a. enthusiastic
b. apathetic
c. laughable
d. helpless

7. savoir-faire
a. injustice
b. tactlessness
c. profitability
d. renown

8. gargantuan
a. tiny
b. summery
c. soft
d. flighty

9. ecumenical
a. lofty
b. evasive
c. parochial
d. amateur

10. ambivalent
a. dubious
b. rash
c. definable
d. unequivocal

11. lampoon
a. homage
b. satire
c. parody
d. variation

12. malleable
a. inflexible
b. affirmative
c. dense
d. yielding

13. beatitude
a. cudgel
b. ugliness
c. tension
d. despair

14. philistine
a. puny
b. foreign
c. refined
d. boorish

15. dank
a. deserted
b. arid
c. impulsive
d. soaked

16. malcontent
a. unruly
b. disgruntled
c. satisfied
d. fugitive

17. truckle
a. glide
b. wallow
c. resign
d. defy

18. bane
a. solace
b. ruin
c. permission
d. halt

19. inchoate
a. naked
b. developed
c. conforming
d. immature

20. prolix
a. distant
b. verbose
c. succinct
d. tyrannical

Completing the Sentence *From the following list of words, choose the one that best completes each of the sentences below. Write the word in the space provided.*

malcontent	**imbue**	**de facto**	**remand**
philistine	**heyday**	**aberration**	**cataclysm**

1. Through examples rather than with words, the scoutmaster managed to
_____ the troop with worthy ideas and aspirations.

2. In order to avoid any further violence, the neighboring states quickly
recognized the _____ government established by
the military leaders.

3. I feel sorry for the _____ who always harp on the negative
rather than the positive aspects of any situation.

R

4. In their _____ transatlantic passenger ships offered luxury unequaled on the seven seas.

5. That one unfortunate reaction should be viewed as a(n) _____ rather than as an example of his customary behavior.

Interesting Derivations

From the following list of words, choose the one that best completes each of the sentences below. Write the word in the space provided.

gargantuan	**kudos**	**nepotism**	**nemesis**
picaresque	**ecumenical**	**prolix**	**inchoate**

1. The adjective _____ comes from the Greek word meaning *encompassing all of the known world.*

2. The name of the "hero" of François Rabelais's famous novel, a character with an astounding capacity for food and pleasure, is the source of the English adjective _____ .

3. A bit of British university slang, derived from the Greek word for *glory* or *honor*, is preserved in the English word _____ .

4. Since, throughout history, powerful leaders have tended to favor their relatives and close personal friends, it is not surprising to find that the word _____ comes from the Latin word for *nephew.*

5. The English adjective _____ is derived from the Spanish noun meaning *rascal* or *rogue.*

Word Families

A. *On the line provided, write a **noun** form for each of the following words.*

EXAMPLE: cantankerous—**cantankerousness**

1. opt _____
2. ambivalent _____
3. fastidious _____
4. malleable _____
5. queasy _____
6. refractory _____
7. prolix _____
8. inveigle _____

84

9. fetid _____

10. dank _____

B. *On the line provided, write an* **adjective** *related to each of the following words.*

EXAMPLE: hedonism—**hedonistic**

1. cataclysm _____

2. bathos _____

3. beatitude _____

4. aberration _____

5. tautology _____

6. opt _____

Filling the Blanks *Encircle the pair of words that best complete the meaning of each of the following passages.*

1. In the spring of that year, bands of marauding Goths broke into the province, _____ the governor in his own capital, and committed such _____ that the economy of the region did not recover for a generation.
   a. beleaguered . . . depredations   c. debauched . . . tautologies
   b. lampooned . . . peccadillos   d. remanded . . . prototypes

2. Though the delightfully roguish adventures of Gil Blas provided the _____ for the kind of _____ novel much admired in the 18th century, the form did not achieve maturity until the writings of Henry Fielding and Tobias Smollett.
   a. éclat . . . ecumenical   c. prototype . . . picaresque
   b. syndrome . . . gargantuan   d. harbinger . . . lackluster

3. Richard Wagner considered the average operagoer of his day a blatant _____ , to whose benighted musical tastes he would in no way _____ .
   a. protégé . . . truckle   c. sycophant . . . opt
   b. hedonist . . . remand   d. philistine . . . pander

4. At the court of an autocratic ruler, free speech is usually replaced by the obsequious twaddle of self-seeking toadies and _____ , eager to get ahead by _____ to the opinions of their all-powerful master.
   a. lagniappes . . . debauching   c. malcontents . . . lampooning
   b. sycophants . . . truckling   d. harbingers . . . pandering

Analogies   *In each of the following, choose the item that best completes the comparison.*

1. inveigle is to **flattery** as
a. cozen is to encouragement
b. browbeat is to intimidation
c. reassure is to censure
d. cajole is to criticism

2. bathos is to **maudlin** as
a. obloquy is to complimentary
b. empathy is to callous
c. persiflage is to picaresque
d. casuistry is to specious

3. aficionado is to **fervid** as
a. pundit is to apathetic
b. sycophant is to caustic
c. connoisseur is to discriminating
d. pessimist is to sanguine

4. mule is to **refractory** as
a. pig is to indolent
b. horse is to iconoclastic
c. fox is to maladroit
d. elephant is to oblivious

5. tautology is to **redundant** as
a. lampoon is to prolix
b. vignette is to noisome
c. homily is to incoherent
d. solecism is to erroneous

6. virtuoso is to **éclat** as
a. gallant is to panache
b. proselyte is to insouciance
c. harbinger is to verisimilitude
d. klutz is to tact

7. bilious is to **queasy** as
a. quizzical is to content
b. contumelious is to elated
c. portentous is to alarmed
d. ambivalent is to sleepy

8. inchoate is to **form** as
a. ineffable is to size
b. chimerical is to substance
c. ecumenical is to scope
d. sacrosanct is to duration

9. midget is to **minuscule** as
a. fait accompli is to abortive
b. dictum is to risible
c. volte-face is to waggish
d. colossus is to gargantuan

10. prude is to **fastidious** as
a. philistine is to crass
b. prodigy is to lackluster
c. incubus is to prurient
d. hedonist is to malcontent

Shades of Meaning   *Read each sentence carefully. Then encircle the item that best completes the sentence below it.*

When joke after joke met with dead silence, the comedian began seriously
to doubt whether the audience was at all risible.   (2)

1. The word **risible** in line 2 most nearly means
a. laughable
b. ludicrous
c. droll
d. inclined to laugh

"He had often noticed that six month's oblivion amounts to newspaper death,
and that resurrection is rare. Nothing is easier, if a man wants it, than rest,   (2)
profound as the grave."   (Henry Adams, *The Education of Henry Adams*)

2. In line 1 the word **oblivion** is used to mean
a. forgetfulness
b. unawareness
c. being forgotten
d. insensibility

Beleaguered by American and French forces on land and at sea, British
general Lord Cornwallis had no choice but to surrender his encircled   (2)
army to General George Washington at Yorktown in October of 1781.

3. The best definition for the word **Beleaguered** in line 1 is
a. Outnumbered   b. Troubled   c. Defeated   d. Surrounded

Besides inventing the lens that bears his name, French physicist
Augustin-Jean Fresnel (1788–1827) investigated the laws governing the
interference of polarized light.

(2)

4. The word **polarized** in line 3 is used to mean
    a. physically alienated   c. evenly split
    b. vibrating in a pattern   d. completely estranged

The summer saw hundreds of volunteers in towns along the rain-swollen
Mississippi work around-the-clock, shoring up river levees with sandbags
in a desperate effort to hold back the cataclysm.

(2)

5. In line 3 the word **cataclysm** most nearly means
    a. deluge   b. upheaval   c. catastrophe   d. disaster

**Filling
the Blanks**
    *Encircle the pair of words that best complete the
meaning of each of the following passages.*

1. "You may consider me a narrow-minded prude," I replied, "but I can see
no redeeming social or artistic value in this book. Indeed, it appears to
_____ exclusively to the _____ interests of
the reader."
    a. inveigle . . . bibulous   c. pander . . . prurient
    b. condescend . . . eleemosynary   d. opt . . . philistine

2. Boss Tweed and his cronies in Tammany Hall were as _____
as hungry sharks, and the _____ they committed on the
public treasury left New York City in severe financial straits.
    a. supine . . . aberrations   c. effete . . . peccadilloes
    b. rapacious . . . depredations   d. maladroit . . . lucubrations

3. Though I remembered him as somewhat awkward and _____ ,
he handled that ticklish social problem with all the _____ of
a born diplomat.
    a. lackluster . . . folderol   c. mellifluous . . . prescience
    b. queasy . . . gamut   d. maladroit . . . savoir-faire

4. Though King Edward VII is often pictured as nothing more than an effete
_____ , with appetites as _____ as his
physique, he was in fact an intelligent, knowledgeable, and perceptive
observer of the European scene.
    a. hedonist . . . gargantuan   c. pundit . . . philistine
    b. harbinger . . . fetid   d. mountebank . . . dank

5. Because her work flouted the canons of classical ballet, Isadora Duncan
soon came to be regarded as an artistic _____ to whom
nothing was _____ .
    a. poltroon . . . ambivalent   c. persona . . . cognate
    b. aficionado . . . internecine   d. iconoclast . . . sacrosanct

Unit   10

Group A

acumen	**dissimulate**
adjudicate	**empirical**
anachronism	**flamboyant**
apocryphal	**fulsome**
disparity	**immolate**

Pronunciation *Match each of the words contained in Group A with its phonetic transcription. Write the appropriate word in the space given.*

1. flam 'boi ənt   _____

2. a 'kyü mən   _____

3. em 'pir i kəl   _____

4. ə 'pok rə fəl   _____

5. di 'sim yə lāt   _____

6. 'fūl səm   _____

7. ə 'jüd i kāt   _____

8. dis 'par ə tē   _____

9. ə 'nak rə niz əm   _____

10. 'im ə lāt   _____

Definition *Choose the word from Group A that most nearly corresponds to each of the definitions below. Write the word in the blank space at the right of the definition and then in the illustrative phrase below it.*

1. (*v.*) to act as judge in a matter; to settle through the use of a judge or legal tribunal   _____

   agreed to _____ the dispute

2. (*adj.*) offensively insincere or excessive; disgusting, sickening   _____

   _____ praise

3. (*n.*) keenness of insight; quickness or accuracy of judgment   _____

   possessed remarkable _____ in matters of business

4. (*v.*) to hide or disguise one's true thoughts, feelings, or intentions   _____

   was able to _____ my anger

5. (*n.*) a chronological misplacing of events, objects, customs, or persons in regard to each other _____

the _____ of Napoleon using a computer

6. (*adj.*) derived from, dependent upon, or guided by practical experience, observation, or experiment, rather than by theory; so verifiable _____

based on purely _____ data

7. (*adj.*) of doubtful or questionable authenticity _____

a(n) _____ story

8. (*n.*) a difference or inequality in age, rank, degree, amount, or quality; a dissimilarity, unlikeness _____

the great _____ between the rich and the poor

9. (*adj.*) highly elaborate or ornate; vividly colored; strikingly brilliant or bold _____

the bird's _____ plumage

10. (*v.*) to kill as a sacrifice, especially by fire; to destroy or renounce for the sake of another _____

_____ the victims

Group B

imperceptible	**nihilism**
lackey	**patrician**
liaison	**propitiate**
monolithic	**sic**
mot juste	**sublimate**

Pronunciation *Match each of the words contained in Group B with its phonetic transcription. Write the appropriate word in the space given.*

1. im pər ′sep tə bəl _____

2. ′səb lə māt _____

3. mō ′zhüst _____

4. ′lak ē _____

5. ′nī əl iz əm _____

6. pə ′trish ən _____

7. sik _____

8. ′lē ə zon _____

9. mon ə ′lith ik _____

10. prō ′pish ē āt _____

Definition   *Choose the word from Group B that most nearly corresponds to each of the definitions below. Write the word in the blank space at the right of the definition and then in the illustrative phrase below it.*

1. (*v.*) to redirect the energy of a biological or instinctual impulse into a higher or more acceptable channel   _____

learned to _____ such impulses

2. (*n.*) the most suitable or exact word or expression   _____

sought for the _____

3. (*v.*) to make someone or something favorably inclined towards oneself; to conciliate, satisfy, or appease   _____

_____ the angry gods

4. (*adj.*) extremely slight; incapable of being perceived by the senses or the mind   _____

by _____ gradations

5. (*n.*) a uniformed male servant; a servile follower   _____

surrounded by servants and _____

6. (*n.*) a total rejection of existing laws, institutions, and moral values; extreme radicalism   _____

the revolutionary's _____

7. (*n.*) the contact or means of communication between groups; someone acting as such a contact; any close relationship; a thickening or binding agent used in cooking   _____

acted as the _____ between school and community

8. (*adj.*) characterized by massiveness, solidness, and total uniformity   _____

a(n) _____ social structure

9. (*adv.*) thus so; intentionally written so   _____

e.e. cummings [_____]

10. (*n.*) a member of the ruling class; a person of high or noble rank or of prominent social standing; belonging to, befitting, or characteristic of such a person   _____

one of the great _____ families of England

Completing the Sentence   *Choose the word for this unit that best completes each of the following sentences. Write it in the space given.*

1. We need not try actively to _____ the opponents of our candidate, but we can certainly take reasonable precautions to avoid antagonizing them.

2. The claims of the surviving victims of last summer's awful airline crash will be _____ by an international commission.

3. A major political party in the United States represents a coalition of many different forces, rather than a(n) _____ structure.

4. Though I believed their promises at first, I soon came to realize the great _____ between their words and their deeds.

5. During the early years of the Roman Republic, plebeians vied bitterly with _____ for political dominance.

6. One would expect such _____ behavior from an attention-seeking celebrity, not from a reputedly stodgy professor of English.

7. It is one thing to spin out ingenious theories; it is quite another to find _____ confirmation for them.

8. Having the inhabitants of Pompeii react to a gladitorial spectacle as if they were watching Monday Night Football struck me as the most ludicrous _____ in the whole miniseries.

9. The company's profits increased remarkably last year, thanks mainly to the new president's exceptional business _____ .

10. I know you're trying to curry favor with the boss, but must you greet each and every one of his bright ideas with such _____ flattery?

11. The sexual drive can be channeled into antisocial forms of behavior or _____ into loftier, more worthwhile endeavors.

12. Their blanket rejection of the standards and values on which our society is founded seems to be little short of senseless _____ .

13. The able auctioneer acknowledged bids from the audience that were so discreet as to be _____ to the untrained eye.

14. During the campaign in West Virginia in 1861, Robert E. Lee acted as the _____ between the commanders of the two independent Confederate brigades operating in the area.

15. Although these stories have been widely accepted for many years, we now have ample evidence to show that they are completely _____ .

16. What a shock it was for her to discover the unworthiness of the cause for which she had _____ her youth, her talents, and her hopes of happiness.

17. As the duke's coach drew up, two _____ in splendid livery stepped forth to open the carriage door.

18. Susanna's efforts to _____ her feelings of inadequacy by pretending to be bored and indifferent are a sign of immaturity.

19. Then she leaned toward me and said confidingly, "Between you and I [_____], I didn't believe a word he said."

20. In calling Tom a "stinker," I may not have been too refined, but in view of his disgraceful conduct, I think I applied the _____ .

Synonyms *Choose the word for this unit that is most nearly **the same** as each of the following groups of expressions. Write it in the space given.*

1. fictitious, mythical, spurious, bogus _____

2. observed, experiential; pragmatic _____

3. a discrepancy, incongruity, difference _____

4. minimal, slight; undetectable _____

5. an aristocrat, peer; noble, highborn _____

6. to rechannel, redirect; to elevate _____

7. insight, perspicacity, shrewdness, acuity _____

8. showy, ostentatious; ornate, florid _____

9. to dissemble, pretend; to misrepresent _____

10. a footman; a toady, flunky, hanger-on _____

11. to appease; to placate, mollify _____

12. excessive, inordinate; repulsive _____

13. to sacrifice; to slay, kill _____

14. to arbitrate, referee, mediate _____

15. an intermediary, channel, contact _____

16. undifferentiated, massive, dense _____

17. total repudiation of the Establishment _____

18. thus, so _____

19. the right word _____

20. a chronological error _____

Antonyms *Choose the word for this unit that is most nearly **opposite** in meaning to each of the following groups of expressions. Write it in the space given.*

1. a peasant, commoner, plebeian _____

2. conspicuous, noticeable; flagrant _____

3. authentic, genuine, true _____

4. a similarity, likeness, congruity _____

5. to estrange, alienate; to provoke, annoy _____

6. diversified, variform, multifarious _____

7. staid, sedate, decorous, seemly, sober _____

8. a lord, liege; an employer, boss _____

9. theoretical, hypothetical, conjectural _____

10. a misnomer, misusage, malapropism _____

11. understated, muted, restrained; agreeable _____

12. to show one's true feelings, reveal _____

13. ignorance, stupidity, obtuseness _____

14. to save, rescue, preserve _____

15. conservatism _____

Choosing the Right Word *Circle the **boldface** word that more satisfactorily completes each of the following sentences.*

1. There is probably nothing worse than having (**patrician, apocryphal**) tastes on an income better suited to the lifestyle of a pauper.

2. No country can survive the combined threat of foreign invasion and domestic insurrection unless it is governed by leaders possessing extraordinary political (**acumen, disparity**).

3. The main character in the comedy is a bumbling inventor who has accidentally transported himself into the past, there to suffer the misadventures of a hapless (**lackey, anachronism**).

4. It is only when she has a large and appreciative audience that she evinces such a "noble" readiness for self-(**nihilism, immolation**).

5. When a small sum is involved, the cost of (**adjudication, dissimulation**) can exceed the amount of the award.

6. When you say that Fred has a talent for (**disparity, dissimulation**), what you really mean is that he is an out-and-out phony.

7. He is so concerned with words that he seems to think the only thing that is needed to deal with a problem is to find the (**mot juste, anachronism**) to describe it.

8. In a pluralistic democracy, such as the United States, there is little chance that a (**flamboyant, monolithic**) public opinion will ever develop on any controversial issue.

9. We are not suggesting that students should run the school, but is it too much to ask that the faculty and administration maintain a sympathetic (**nihilism, liaison**) with the young people under their authority?

10. While I agree that there are imperfections in our society, I simply cannot accept his (**patrician, nihilistic**) belief that the entire heritage of the past must be discarded.

11. In his campaign speech he said, "My opponent has flaunted [(**sic, mot juste**)] all of the principles of sound fiscal management."

12. I never cease to wonder at the (**liaison, disparity**) between what people aspire to do and what they are equipped to do by natural endowment and training.

13. Though Plato's approach to philosophy often seems somewhat mystical, Aristotle's is decidedly (**empirical, fulsome**).

14. Those solemn religious ceremonies are intended to protect the tribe from disasters by (**propitiating, adjudicating**) the gods who control natural phenomena.

15. He expressed the idea that genius in any field represents a special kind of (**adjudication, sublimation**) of capacities, drives, and needs that are in all of us.

16. Because deadly carbon monoxide gas can be neither seen nor smelled, its presence is practically (**empirical, imperceptible**).

17. The story about Bunker Hill and "Don't fire until you see the whites of their eyes" may be (**monolithic, apocryphal**), but I like it, and I'm going to continue believing it.

18. It's no wonder he's got such a swelled head when all those (**patricians, lackeys**) that tag along after him do nothing but sing his praises.

19. American voters may be attracted and amused by a (**patrician, flamboyant**) personality, but they seem to prefer more sober and conventional types when making their choice for high public office.

20. There seemed no point in the author's gratuitous use of such (**fulsome, apocryphal**) language other than to offend the taste of the reader.

Unit 11

Group A

apostate	effusive
bravado	euphoria
consensus	gothic
constrict	impasse
dichotomy	lugubrious

Pronunciation *Match each of the words contained in Group A with its phonetic transcription. Write the appropriate word in the space given.*

1. i ′fyü siv _____

2. lù ′gü brē əs _____

3. ′goth ik _____

4. brə ′vä dō _____

5. ′im pas _____

6. dī ′kot ə mē _____

7. yü ′fōr ē ə _____

8. kən ′strikt _____

9. ə ′pos tāt _____

10. kən ′sen səs _____

Definition *Choose the word from Group A that most nearly corresponds to each of the definitions below. Write the word in the blank space at the right of the definition and then in the illustrative phrase below it.*

1. (*n.*) one who forsakes his or her religion, party, or cause; (*adj.*) renouncing or abandoning an allegiance _____

receive the _____ back into the fold

2. (*adj.*) highly demonstrative; unrestrained _____

a(n) _____ welcome

3. (*n.*) a dead end; a position from which there is no escape; a problem to which there is no solution _____

a hopeless _____

4. (*n.*) a feeling of great happiness or well-being, often with no objective basis _____

in a state of _____

5. (*adj.*) sad, mournful, or gloomy, especially to an exaggerated or ludicrous degree

_____

a(n) _____ tale of woe

6. (*n.*) a display of false or assumed courage

_____

sheer _____

7. (*n.*) a collective or general agreement of opinion, feeling, or thinking

_____

reached a(n) _____ at last

8. (*n.*) a division into two contradictory or mutually exclusive parts; a branching or forking in an ancestral line

_____

the basic _____ between theory and practice

9. (*v.*) to make smaller or narrower, draw together, squeeze; to stop or cause to falter

_____

_____ by a tight collar

10. (*adj.*) characterized by or emphasizing a gloomy setting and grotesque or violent events; such a literary or artistic style; a type of medieval architecture

_____

a(n) _____ novel

Group B

metamorphosis	**quagmire**
mystique	**quixotic**
non sequitur	**raconteur**
parlous	**sine qua non**
punctilio	**vendetta**

Pronunciation *Match each of the words contained in Group B with its phonetic transcription. Write the appropriate word in the space given.*

1. kwik ′sot ik _____

2. non ′sek wi tər _____

3. ven ′det ə _____

4. ′pär ləs _____

5. rak on ′tər _____

6. met ə ′môr fə sis _____

7. ′kwag mīr _____

8. sin ə kwä ′nōn _____

9. pəŋk ′til ē ō _____

10. mi ′stēk _____

Definition   *Choose the word from Group B that most nearly corresponds to each of the definitions below. Write the word in the blank space at the right of the definition and then in the illustrative phrase below it.*

1. (*n.*) a minute detail of conduct or procedure; an instant of time _____

the _____ of a perfectionist

2. (*n.*) a complete transformation, as if by magic _____

the _____ of tadpoles into frogs

3. (*n.*) a person who tells stories and anecdotes with great skill _____

a noted _____

4. (*n.*) an essential or indispensable element or condition _____

the _____ of lasting happiness

5. (*adj.*) extravagantly or romantically idealistic; visionary without regard to practical considerations _____

a(n) _____ turn of mind

6. (*n.*) a prolonged feud, often between two families, characterized by retaliatory acts of revenge; any act motivated by vengeance _____

a literary _____

7. (*n.*) an inference or conclusion that does not follow logically from the facts or premises _____

an argument undermined by _____

8. (*n.*) an aura or attitude of mystery or veneration surrounding something or someone _____

the Kennedy _____

9. (*n.*) soft, soggy mud or slush; a difficult or entrapping situation _____

a treacherous _____

10. (*adj.*) full of danger or risk, perilous _____

a(n) _____ undertaking

Completing the Sentence   *Choose the word for this unit that best completes each of the following sentences. Write it in the space given.*

1. One look at the coach's _____ face, and I knew that all our misgivings about the outcome of the game had been borne out.

2. Though everyone in our club agreed that we had a problem, there was no group _____ on how to solve it.

3. Not until later did I realize that their _____ expressions of interest in our welfare were insincere and self-serving.

4. The man was a skilled _____ whose repertory of amusing anecdotes was seemingly inexhaustible.

5. You cannot duck your responsibility for negotiating an agreement simply by announcing that you have reached a hopeless _____ .

6. The speakers said that they could see little hope for world peace unless something could be done to bridge the _____ between the "have" and the "have-not" nations.

7. The rugged landscape, with the severe vertical lines of the mountains in the background, lent an air of _____ gloom to the entire scene.

8. The police investigation established that the knifing victim was not an innocent bystander but the target of a gangland _____ .

9. It is true that modern military power requires great industrial resources, but to conclude from this that industrialized nations are inherently militaristic is an obvious _____ .

10. As the disappointing results of the poll filtered in, the candidate sank into a(n) _____ of doubts about the future.

11. The mood of _____ brought about by our extraordinary good fortune caused us to relax our usual alertness.

12. His challenge to fight was pure _____ ; inwardly he hoped that no one would take him on.

13. How can you concern yourself with the _____ of protocol when your whole world is collapsing about your ears?

14. The new book contains a rare insight into the _____ of the bullring and the complex of almost religious attitudes that surround that ancient blood sport.

15. It took Rome centuries to achieve her miraculous _____ from a minor city-state on the banks of the Tiber to the leading power in the Mediterranean world.

16. Although it may be true that hard work does not guarantee success, it is certainly a(n) _____ for doing well in any endeavor.

17. When he came to the throne, Julian the _____ renounced Christianity and began a vigorous campaign to reestablish paganism as the official religion of the Roman Empire.

18. To achieve an hourglass figure, fashionable ladies of the 19th century employed tight-fitting corsets to _____ their waistlines.

19. Each episode in the silent-movie serial *The Perils of Pauline* ended with the heroine facing another _____ predicament.

20. Every great President must combine various roles—the practical politician, the masterful intellectual, the tough administrator, the persuasive advocate —and at least a touch of the _____ visionary.

Synonyms   *Choose the word for this unit that is most nearly **the same** as each of the following groups of expressions. Write it in the space given.*

1. a fine point, nicety _____

2. fanciful, impractical; utopian _____

3. doleful, melancholy, dismal, dolorous _____

4. hazardous, perilous, risky, dangerous _____

5. a deadlock, stand-off, stalemate _____

6. elation, bliss, ecstasy, rapture _____

7. unanimity, concord, accord, harmony _____

8. a schism, division, bifurcation _____

9. a blood feud, rivalry _____

10. gloomy, grotesque; sinister, eerie _____

11. gushy, lavish, demonstrative _____

12. a renegade, defector, turncoat _____

13. a storyteller, anecdotist _____

14. swagger, bluster, braggadocio _____

15. a fen, marsh, bog, morass _____

16. an aura, charisma _____

17. a necessity, requisite, desideratum _____

18. a change, transformation, makeover _____

19. to contract, squeeze; to curb, restrain _____

20. an illogical inference, unsound conclusion _____

Antonyms *Choose the word for this unit that is most nearly*
***opposite** in meaning to each of the following groups of*
expressions. Write it in the space given.

1. merry, jovial; hilarious, funny _____

2. melancholy, depression, gloom _____

3. safe, secure, risk-free _____

4. realistic, down-to-earth, pragmatic _____

5. to enlarge, dilate, expand _____

6. bedrock, solid footing, terra firma _____

7. a true believer, loyalist _____

8. something that is optional _____

9. dissension, discord, disagreement _____

10. uniformity, oneness _____

11. restrained, reserved, muted, subdued _____

12. true courage, mettle, bravery, pluck _____

Choosing the *Circle the **boldface** word that more satisfactorily*
Right Word *completes each of the following sentences.*

1. As we learned to understand each other's needs and aspirations, a sort of unspoken (**consensus, impasse**) developed that enabled us to work together harmoniously.

2. Does it seem paradoxical that, like many other great comedians, she goes about with a characteristically (**lugubrious, parlous**) expression on her face?

3. Spacesuits are designed to afford astronauts maximum protection without unduly (**constricting, dichotomizing**) their freedom of movement.

4. Even though their son had abandoned the religion in which he had been brought up, his parents never thought of him as an (**apostate, impasse**).

5. Though your efforts to enact a program of ecological reform in the face of strong opposition were (**quixotic, gothic**) and foredoomed to failure, they were wonderfully inspiring.

6. There are very few world problems that can be understood in terms of a simple (**euphoria, dichotomy**) of right and wrong.

7. I wanted a direct, factual explanation of what had happened, but all I got was emotional (**effusions, quagmires**) describing in painful detail how much they had suffered.

8. There is no point in trying to decide exactly which of the factors is most important for victory in the election; every one of them is a (**non sequitur, sine qua non**).

9. Despite the grave risks that the rescue attempt would entail, there was no shortage of volunteers for the (**parlous, effusive**) undertaking.

10. Our thesis was that at this stage in their history Americans must eschew the (**dichotomy, mystique**) of "manly" force and violence and develop new ideals of social cooperation.

11. "I have followed Cupid's jack-o'-lantern and find myself in a (**consensus, quagmire**) at last."

12. The new assistant dean's adherence to every (**impasse, punctilio**) in the Student Code alienated both the faculty and the student body.

13. Perhaps her volunteering to undertake the mission was mere (**bravado, consensus**), but the fact remains that she did accomplish everything that was expected of her.

14. It's laughable of you to think that you are an accomplished (**raconteur, apostate**) just because you have memorized an assortment of old jokes and can do a few feeble impersonations.

15. Their analysis of the problem seemed to me extremely fallacious—full of false assumptions, dubious generalizations, and (**constrictions, non sequiturs**).

16. In *Romeo and Juliet,* the hero's tragic death comes as the result of a long-standing (**vendetta, bravado**) between his family and Juliet's.

17. The ordeal of the Civil War (**apostasized, metamorphosed**) Lincoln from an obscure small-town lawyer into a historical personality of universal appeal.

18. It is impossible for me to convey the intensity of emotion that I felt at that (**lugubrious, euphoric**) moment when I learned I had won the scholarship.

19. For a long time we lived in the illusion that "everything would come out all right," but inevitably we arrived at the (**vendetta, impasse**) where we had to face realities and make painful decisions.

20. There, are times when I like to read a (**gothic, parlous**) tale of gloomy castles, mysterious strangers, and unhappy love affairs.

Unit 12

Group A

apposite	execrable
augur	impinge
bilk	labyrinth
charisma	narcissism
debilitate	niggardly

Pronunciation *Match each of the words contained in Goup A with its phonetic transcription. Write the appropriate word in the space given.*

1. 'när sə siz əm _____

2. di 'bil ə tāt _____

3. 'ek si krə bəl _____

4. bilk _____

5. 'ap ə zit _____

6. 'nig ərd lē _____

7. kə 'riz mə _____

8. im 'pinj _____

9. 'ô ger _____

10. 'lab ə rinth _____

Definition *Choose the word from Group A that most nearly corresponds to each of the definitions below. Write the word in the blank space at the right of the definition and then in the illustrative phrase below it.*

1. (*n.*) excessive self-love; absorption in oneself _____

repelled by his _____

2. (*n.*) a bewildering maze; any confusing or complicated situation _____

a subterranean _____

3. (*n.*) a prophet or seer; (*v.*) to predict, foreshadow _____

did not _____ well for the future

4. (*v.*) to strike against or collide with violently; to encroach or obtrude upon; to make an impression upon _____

_____ upon our rights

5. (*adj.*) appropriate; suitable; apt   _____

    gave a(n) _____ answer to her question

6. (*adj.*) stingy; meanly small or insufficient   _____

    rather _____ with your advice and guidance

7. (*adj.*) utterly detestable, hateful, or abhorrent; extremely inferior   _____

    crude and _____ conduct

8. (*v.*) to defraud, cheat, or swindle; to evade payment of; to frustrate, thwart   _____

    _____ the credulous old man

9. (*n.*) the special personal magnetism that makes an individual exceptionally appealing to other people; a divinely bestowed gift or power   _____

    the _____ of a born leader

10. (*v.*) to make weak or feeble   _____

    _____ by illness

Group B

pastiche	**vagary**
precarious	**viable**
rapport	**xenophobia**
utilitarian	**zany**
vacuous	**zealot**

Pronunciation   *Match each of the words contained in Group B with its phonetic transcription. Write the appropriate word in the space given.*

1. 'vak yü əs   _____

2. 'zā nē   _____

3. pas 'tēsh   _____

4. pri 'kâr ē əs   _____

5. 'zel ət   _____

6. ra 'pôr   _____

7. 'vā gə rē   _____

8. zen ə 'fō bē ə   _____

9. yü til ə 'târ ē ən   _____

10. 'vī ə bəl   _____

Definition   *Choose the word from Group B that most nearly
corresponds to each of the definitions below. Write the
word in the blank space at the right of the definition and
then in the illustrative phrase below it.*

1. (*n.*) an unpredictable, erratic, or seemingly
purposeless action, occurrence, or notion   _____

the endless _____ of the fashion world

2. (*n.*) a fanatical partisan; an ardent follower   _____

religious _____

3. (*n.*) undue or unreasonable fear, hatred, or contempt
of foreigners or strangers or of what is foreign or
strange   _____

blinded by _____

4. (*adj.*) devoid of matter, substance, or meaning;
lacking ideas or intelligence; purposeless   _____

a(n) _____ stare

5. (*adj.*) capable of living or developing under normal
circumstances   _____

a(n) _____ solution to the company's problems

6. (*adj.*) clownish or funny in a crazy, bizarre, or
ludicrous way; (*n.*) one who plays the clown   _____

the _____ antics of the Marx Brothers

7. (*n.*) a close and harmonious relationship   _____

established a _____ with her clients

8. (*n.*) a dramatic, musical, or literary work made up of
bits and pieces from other sources; a hodgepodge   _____

a(n) _____ of familiar show tunes

9. (*adj.*) stressing practicality over other considerations;
relating to the belief that what is good or desirable is
determined purely by its usefulness   _____

a(n) _____ philosopher

10. (*adj.*) very uncertain or unsure; dangerous or risky   _____

a(n) _____ balance of power

**Completing
the Sentence**   *Choose the word for this unit that best completes each
of the following sentences. Write it in the space given.*

1. "Any organization that is able to survive and prosper in these trying times

has indeed proven itself _____ ," she observed.

2. Our party can use the support of ardent young _____ , but we also need the help of older and cooler heads that do not regard a political campaign as a great moral crusade.

3. I cannot accept a purely _____ view of life that ignores such aspects of human experience as beauty, love, and humor.

4. Attacked from all sides by superior forces, the army found itself in a(n) _____ , if not totally untenable, position.

5. When we asked the climbers why they wanted to scale the mountain, they gave the _____ reply, "Because it's there."

6. Her consistent attitude of hostility toward any cultural tradition different from her own cannot be excused by calling it _____ .

7. Oscar Wilde's famous epigram that "Self-love is the beginning of a life-long romance" is a clever comment on _____ .

8. The fumble by our quarterback on the opening kickoff, followed by a 15-yard penalty against us, did not _____ well for our team.

9. Luxury and self-indulgence _____ the once vigorous Roman people and led to the fall of the empire.

10. We cannot say with any confidence how long this trip will take us, because our progress is dependent upon the _____ of the weather.

11. Only later did we come to realize that there was a serious purpose behind his apparently frivolous remarks and _____ behavior.

12. As I lay there, drifting off to sleep, suddenly the sound of a very loud, very raucous, and very obnoxious television commercial _____ on my ears.

13. Only after living and working in Washington for many years were we able to find our way through the vast _____ of governmental departments and agencies.

14. By filing false claims over a period of many years, the pair attempted to _____ the insurance company of large sums of money.

15. Instead of sentimentalizing about the passing of rural and small-town America, we must work to achieve an effective _____ with our modern urban environment.

16. We recognize the need for vigorous criticism in a political campaign, but we will certainly not tolerate that kind of _____ character assassination.

17. His _____ remarks revealed how little he really knew about political economy.

12

18. Although I am not one of the more prosperous members of the community, my contributions to charity are by no means _____ .

19. Some leaders have such great personal _____ that they inspire an attitude akin to religious veneration in their followers.

20. Since the play is essentially a(n) _____ of devices and ideas drawn from many different sources, it lacks the consistency and cohesiveness of the writer's other works.

Synonyms   *Choose the word for this unit that is most nearly the **same** in meaning as each of the following groups of expressions. Write it in the space given.*

1. a medley, patchwork, melange, potpourri   _____

2. a seer, oracle; to bode, foreshadow   _____

3. to dupe, swindle, cheat, defraud, cozen   _____

4. inane, insipid, fatuous; void, empty   _____

5. a caprice, whim, quirk   _____

6. a fanatic, extremist   _____

7. egotism, conceit, vanity, amour propre   _____

8. practicable, workable, feasible   _____

9. relevant, pertinent, apt, material, germane   _____

10. to encroach, horn in, affect   _____

11. perilous, risky; dubious; ticklish   _____

12. comical, daffy; a buffoon, clown   _____

13. to enervate, sap, exhaust, enfeeble   _____

14. tightfisted, penny-pinching, mean   _____

15. odious, abominable, reprehensible   _____

16. a maze, tangle; a mystery, enigma   _____

17. a bond, tie, affinity, understanding   _____

18. magnetism, appeal, charm, mystique   _____

19. practical, functional, pragmatic   _____

20. provinciality, parochialism, chauvinism   _____

Antonyms *Choose the word for this unit that is most nearly*
***opposite** in meaning to each of the following groups of
expressions. Write it in the space given.*

1. generous, bountiful, magnanimous _____

2. nonfunctional, ornamental, decorative _____

3. secure, safe, sturdy, firm _____

4. commendable, praiseworthy, meritorious _____

5. incisive, trenchant, perceptive, intelligent _____

6. to strengthen, fortify, invigorate _____

7. sedate, decorous, prim, sober, grave _____

8. irrelevant, immaterial, inappropriate _____

9. unpracticable, unworkable, unfeasible _____

10. a total lack of feeling for _____

Choosing the *Circle the **boldface** word that more satisfactorily*
Right Word *completes each of the following sentences.*

1. Their optimism is so unwavering and so all-encompassing that bad news simply fails to (**impinge, bilk**) on their confidence.

2. Even while stressing, as we must, (**utilitarian, narcissistic**) goals, we cannot afford to ignore ethical and aesthetic values.

3. True patriotism is a positive attitude, as contrasted with the negative orientation of (**charisma, xenophobia**).

4. His idea of (**zany, zealous**) behavior at a party is to wear a lampshade as if it were a hat.

5. Because the speaker before her had defined the topic so narrowly, Sylvia had to revise her notes so that only (**apposite, precarious**) data remained.

6. It was the function of a Roman (**augur, zany**) to divine the wills of the gods through the interpretation of various natural phenomena, including the flight of birds.

7. The disease had such a (**debilitating, zany**) effect upon her constitution that she was unable to return to work for almost a year.

8. Your (**xenophobic, zealous**) enthusiasm must be matched by training and discipline if you are to achieve anything worthwhile.

9. In condemning their (**apposite, execrable**) conduct, let us not assume that we ourselves are completely free of blame.

10. A true work of art must comprise an integrated whole rather than a (**vagary, pastiche**) of discrete or incongruous elements.

11. I have no sympathy for anyone who has allowed himself to be (**impinged, bilked**) by such an obvious get-rich-quick scheme.

12. Anyone who spends so many hours a day primping and preening in front of a mirror can only be considered a blatant (**narcissist, zealot**).

13. When I had lived only a short time in that godforsaken part of the world, I began to realize just how (**vacuous, niggardly**) Nature could sometimes be in bestowing her bounty.

14. Education is not just an impersonal transmission of knowledge from one person to another; it is a living process that requires above all a close (**charisma, rapport**) between teacher and student.

15. With the invading army still far from subdued and so many rival claimants still actively engaged in trying to depose him, the monarch knew that his hold on the throne was at best (**viable, precarious**).

16. How can you be so easily impressed by those (**vacuous, niggardly**) generalizations and clichés?

17. Every President of our country should not only heighten our appreciation of what has been accomplished in the past but also renew our determination to create a more (**precarious, viable**) political and social structure for the future.

18. Succeeding in business is not comparable to advancing along a straight line, but rather to finding one's way through an uncharted, (**labyrinthine, apposite**) passage.

19. What we need now is not (**utilitarian, charismatic**) leadership, however inspiring, but steady, modest, and down-to-earth assistance in defining and achieving our goals.

20. Although I had no desire to wander through a strange town on foot, I was reluctant to trust my person to the (**vagaries, rapports**) of those wild cab drivers.

Review   Units 10–12

Analogies   In each of the following, choose the item that best completes the comparison.

1. astute is to **acumen** as
a. indigent is to wealth
b. diplomatic is to tact
c. clumsy is to skill
d. vacuous is to intelligence

2. judge is to **adjudicate** as
a. lawyer is to propitiate
b. bodyguard is to guide
c. doctor is to sublimate
d. champion is to defend

3. imperceptible is to **notice** as
a. intangible is to touch
b. insoluble is to discern
c. invisible is to sense
d. invariable is to foresee

4. xenophobe is to **strangers** as
a. miser is to money
b. narcissist is to self
c. misogynist is to women
d. glutton is to food

5. parlous is to **danger** as
a. monolithic is to variety
b. precarious is to insecurity
c. fulsome is to restraint
d. quixotic is to practicality

6. gullible is to **bilk** as
a. valiant is to cow
b. confident is to perturb
c. docile is to lead
d. affluent is to impoverish

7. mot juste is to **apposite** as
a. non sequitur is to illogical
b. anachronism is to timely
c. malapropism is to accurate
d. sine qua non is to optional

8. immolate is to **fire** as
a. pulverize is to dust
b. incinerate is to ashes
c. debilitate is to air
d. inundate is to water

9. clown is to **zany** as
a. zealot is to patrician
b. showoff is to flamboyant
c. jester is to lugubrious
d. spy is to effusive

10. niggardly is to **tight fist** as
a. liberal is to open hand
b. quixotic is to green thumb
c. ethical is to light finger
d. execrable is to itching palm

Identification   In each of the following groups, circle the word that is best defined or suggested by the introductory phrase.

1. bogged down in red tape
a. narcissism   b. quagmire   c. rapport   d. acumen

2. the perfect word for the occasion
a. sine qua non   b. nihilism   c. mot juste   d. sublimate

3. settled the dispute
a. dichotomy   b. flamboyant   c. monolithic   d. adjudicate

4. a novel abounding in blood, violence, and weird happenings
a. fulsome   b. apocryphal   c. gothic   d. viable

5. "Foreigners, go home!"
a. xenophobia   b. impasse   c. mystique   d. vacuous

6. a member of the upper crust
a. punctilio   b. patrician   c. augur   d. zany

7. personal magnetism
a. quixotic   b. disparity   c. euphoria   d. charisma

8. a turncoat like the emperor Julian
a. apostate   b. dissimulate   c. non sequitur   d. effusive

R

9. a born storyteller
a. bilk   b. execrable   c. constrict   d. raconteur

10. an unpredictable event
a. vagary   b. bravado   c. lugubrious   d. vendetta

11. a maze of underground passageways
a. consensus   b. labyrinth   c. apposite   d. parlous

12. an official representing the local union at national headquarters
a. anachronism   b. debilitate   c. liaison   d. niggardly

13. a bit of this and a bit of that
a. propitiate   b. sic   c. precarious   d. pastiche

14. a fanatic
a. lackey   b. impinge   c. zealot   d. imperceptible

15. a magical transformation
a. metamorphosis   b. immolate   c. utilitarian   d. empirical

---

Shades of Meaning   *Read each sentence carefully. Then encircle the item that best completes the sentence below it.*

The merciless Russian winter played an important part in bilking attempts on Moscow both by Napoleon's Grande Armée in 1812 and Hitler's Wehrmacht in 1941.   **(2)**

1. The word **bilking** in line 1 most nearly means
a. cheating   b. thwarting   c. swindling   d. duping

A genealogy of the American Whig party would show a final dichotomy in the 1850s, one branch merging with the newly formed Republican party, the other with the soon-to-be-extinct Know-Nothing party.   **(2)** **(4)**

2. In line 1 the word **dichotomy** is used to mean
a. forking   b. schism   c. bifurcation   d. union

Cosmologists who subscribe to the big bang theory believe that the explosion from which the universe emerged occurred at least 10 billion years ago but lasted only a punctilio.   **(2)**

3. The best definition for the word **punctilio** in line 3 is
a. nicety   b. fine point   c. detail   d. instant

Any chef who would venture oriental dishes must be sure to have stocked in his or her pantry a supply of cornstarch, which is employed as a liaison in the preparation of many common sauces.   **(2)**

4. The word **liaison** in line 3 is used to mean
a. intermediary   b. channel   c. thickener   d. contact

As we drove into the storm we were greeted by a staccato drumming produced by marble-size hailstones impinging upon the rooftop of the car.   **(2)**

5. In line 2 the phrase **impinging upon** most nearly means
a. obtruding   b. encroaching   c. affecting   d. striking

Antonyms

*In each of the following groups, circle the item that is most nearly **opposite** in meaning to the first word in **boldface type.***

1. apocryphal
a. fictitious
b. stolen
c. worthless
d. authentic

2. monolithic
a. old-fashioned
b. trite
c. energetic
d. diversified

3. consensus
a. survey
b. agreement
c. beginning
d. disagreement

4. debilitate
a. invigorate
b. enervate
c. remit
d. injure

5. flamboyant
a. staid
b. obnoxious
c. harmless
d. immense

6. acumen
a. verbosity
b. sharpness
c. artfulness
d. obtuseness

7. lugubrious
a. melancholy
b. hilarious
c. temporary
d. drowsy

8. disparity
a. flaw
b. similarity
c. fusion
d. rationality

9. execrable
a. commendable
b. intentional
c. indisposed
d. intense

10. euphoria
a. charisma
b. narcissism
c. pastiche
d. melancholy

11. patrician
a. noble
b. rural
c. urban
d. plebeian

12. apposite
a. irrelevant
b. meek
c. mutual
d. similar

13. viable
a. wordy
b. truthful
c. unworkable
d. practical

14. quagmire
a. morass
b. defeat
c. bedrock
d. detour

15. niggardly
a. grasping
b. generous
c. uncomfortable
d. pensive

16. mot juste
a. harangue
b. benefit
c. malapropism
d. desideratum

17. zany
a. daffy
b. impromptu
c. decorous
d. complicated

18. vacuous
a. incisive
b. cool
c. decisive
d. elderly

19. constrict
a. reject
b. disturb
c. expand
d. divide

20. quixotic
a. realistic
b. romantic
c. ancient
d. regional

Completing the Sentence

From the following list of words, choose the one that best completes each of the sentences below. Write the word in the space provided.

disparity	**empirical**	**narcissism**	**quagmire**
pastiche	**apposite**	**apocryphal**	**raconteur**

1. I was not pleased to learn that "Washington and the Cherry Tree" is a(n) _____ story.

2. My hypothesis is based solely on the _____ data collected by reliable observers.

3. The wily politician hoped to avoid the _____ of controversial social issues in which his opponent had become extricably mired.

4. A _____ of old plots and new scandals, this soap opera has little chance of catching on with the viewing public.

5. It is sometimes very difficult to tell where self-confidence leaves off and _____ begins.

Interesting Derivations	*From the following list of words, choose the one that best completes each of the sentences below. Write the word in the space provided.*

augur	**labyrinth**	**zealot**	**apostate**
quixotic	**zany**	**gothic**	**patrician**

1. The name of the elaborate complex of passageways and corridors built to house the Minotaur, the Cretan monster eventually slain by Theseus, gives us the English noun _____ .

2. *Gianni (Johnny),* the name usually given to one of the clowns or buffoons in the Italian *commedia dell'arte,* is probably the basis for the English adjective _____ .

3. The name applied to members of a radical, aggressive, and fanatically patriotic Jewish sect in first-century Palestine is the source of the English noun _____ .

4. The name of the hero of Cervantes's famous novel, who was inspired by lofty but quite unobtainable goals, is the source of the English adjective

_____ .

5. The name of the barbarous and fearful Germanic tribe that suddenly swooped down on the Roman Empire during the 3rd century A.D. is still preserved in the English adjective _____ .

Word Families

A. *On the line provided, write a **noun** related to each of the following words.*
EXAMPLE: empirical—**empiricist**

1. sublimate　　　　　　　　_____
2. constrict　　　　　　　　_____
3. apocryphal　　　　　　　　_____
4. monolithic　　　　　　　　_____
5. effusive　　　　　　　　_____
6. viable　　　　　　　　_____

B. *On the line provided, write an* **adjective** *related to each of the following words.*

EXAMPLE: anachronism—**anachronistic**

1. disparity _____

2. nihilism _____

3. euphoria _____

4. punctilio _____

5. charisma _____

6. zealot _____

7. narcissism _____

Filling the Blanks   *Circle the pair of words that best complete the meaning of each of the following passages.*

1. Throughout the 18th and 19th centuries the great _____ houses of England were staffed by a veritable army of servants and _____ , but changes in the British economy since World War I have made it impossible for a modern-day duke or earl to keep such a sizable domestic establishment.

a. patrician . . . lackeys
b. monolithic . . . apostates
c. gothic . . . zealots
d. utilitarian . . . raconteurs

2. As her _____ lover Aeneas fled her embraces in search of his destiny on the wild and desolate shores of Italy, distraught Queen Dido _____ herself on a huge pyre set up for the purpose atop the highest building in Carthage.

a. apocryphal . . . bilked
b. fulsome . . . debilitated
c. apostate . . . immolated
d. execrable . . . adjudicated

3. Some of the anecdotes recounted about famous historical figures are clearly _____ because they contain _____ and other improbable elements that show the stories to have been devised at a much later date.

a. empirical . . . disparities
b. apocryphal . . . anachronisms
c. utilitarian . . . dichotomies
d. apposite . . . non sequiturs

4. When the representatives of labor and management found that they had reached a hopeless _____ in the negotiations for a new contract, they called in an outside mediator to help break the deadlock and _____ the dispute.

a. liaison . . . impinge
b. consensus . . . debilitate
c. rapport . . . dissimulate
d. impasse . . . adjudicate

Analogies *In each of the following, choose the item that best completes the comparison.*

1. quixotic is to **chimerical** as
a. lugubrious is to lachrymose
b. fastidious is to malcontent
c. minuscule is to gargantuan
d. dank is to mellifluous

2. patrician is to **aristocracy** as
a. philistine is to bourgeoisie
b. plebeian is to hoi polloi
c. utilitarian is to proletariat
d. sycophant is to elite

3. quagmire is to **morass** as
a. heyday is to decline
b. kudos is to obloquy
c. bane is to nemesis
d. pundit is to proselyte

4. showoff is to **flamboyant** as
a. nihilist is to hidebound
b. apostate is to loyal
c. poltroon is to valiant
d. skinflint is to niggardly

5. dichotomy is to **two** as
a. disparity is to four
b. liaison is to five
c. affinity is to three
d. consensus is to one

6. raconteur is to **anecdotes** as
a. nitwit is to dictums
b. scholar is to tautologies
c. encomiast is to philippics
d. moralist is to homilies

7. augur is to **birds** as
a. necromancer is to tea leaves
b. medium is to tarot cards
c. haruspex is to entrails
d. mountebank is to poltergeists

8. rogue is to **picaresque** as
a. mnemonic is to allegorical
b. incubus is to gothic
c. apostate is to epistolary
d. pundit is to historical

9. beatitude is to **blissful** as
a. euphoria is to ecstatic
b. despair is to fervid
c. apathy is to disinterested
d. composure is to distraught

10. anachronism is to **time** as
a. malapropism is to tone
b. neologism is to structure
c. solecism is to grammar
d. spoonerism is to accent

Shades of Meaning *Read each sentence carefully. Then encircle the item that best completes the sentence below it.*

In certain cultures shamans are believed to possess a sort of charisma that permits them to heal the sick and even communicate with the spirits of the dead. **(2)**

1. In line 1 the word **charisma** is used to mean
a. personal magnetism
b. charm
c. divine gift
d. mystique

Gradually, we came to see that the champion's every move, though apparently vacuous, was in fact in furtherance of a grand design. **(2)**

2. The word **vacuous** in line 2 most nearly means
a. void
b. fatuous
c. inane
d. purposeless

"People in those old times had convictions; we moderns only have opinions, and it takes more than a mere opinion to erect a Gothic cathedral." **(2)**
(Heinrich Heine, *The French Stage*)

3. The best definition of the word **Gothic** in line 2 is
a. grotesque
b. sinister
c. gloomy
d. medieval-style

The fighting at the Sunken Road during the Battle of Antietam was so sanguine that the site afterward came to be known as Bloody Lane. **(2)**

4. The word **sanguine** in line 2 most nearly means
  a. ruddy
  b. bloody
  c. confident
  d. optimistic

The man whom Edgar Poe appointed his literary executor proved to be a malicious sycophant whose baseless slanders gave rise to myths about Poe that have endured to this day. **(2)**

5. In line 2 the word **sycophant** is used to mean
  a. defamer
  b. toady
  c. flatterer
  d. yes-man

Filling the Blanks *Encircle the pair of words that best complete the meaning of each of the following passages.*

1. When they're in their cups, some of the _____ denizens of the local gin mill become pugnacious, others become sleepy, and still others become teary-eyed and _____ .
  a. hidebound . . . effusive
  b. bilious . . . waggish
  c. bibulous . . . maudlin
  d. malleable . . . contumelious

2. Although one of the most learned men of his time, François Rabelais is best known as a(n) _____ , under the broad, earthy, and often _____ humor of whose tales lie serious discussions of education, politics, religion, and philosophy.
  a. raconteur . . . ribald
  b. polemicist . . . supine
  c. homilist . . . maladroit
  d. virtuoso . . . tendentious

3. Many 18th-century composers merely sketched out the broad outlines of a piece of music and left the details to the taste and discretion of the individual performer. Though this system of composition gives the artist considerable latitude for choice within the _____ of the composer's style, it by no means gives him or her _____ to change the basic structure, design, or mood of the work.
  a. purview . . . pièce de résistance
  b. parameters . . . carte blanche
  c. lexicon . . . fait accompli
  d. matrix . . . mot juste

4. Though human sacrifice was more or less unknown to the Greeks and Romans of ancient times, many of the barbarian tribes along the borders of the classical world customarily _____ their angry gods by _____ prisoners of war or other captives on huge pyres erected in sacred groves or other such places.
  a. bruited . . . debauching
  b. lampooned . . . bowdlerizing
  c. cozened . . . deracinating
  d. propitiated . . . immolating

Unit 13

Group A

accolade	chronic
acerbity	expound
attrition	factionalism
bromide	immaculate
chauvinist	imprecation

Pronunciation Match each of the words contained in Group A with its phonetic transcription. Write the appropriate word in the space given.

1. 'fak shən əl iz əm _____

2. 'ak ə lād _____

3. ek 'spaund _____

4. i 'mak yə lit _____

5. ə 'sər bə tē _____

6. 'shō və nist _____

7. im prə 'kā shən _____

8. ə 'trish ən _____

9. 'kron ik _____

10. 'brō mīd _____

Definition Choose the word from Group A that most nearly corresponds to each of the definitions below. Write the word in the blank space provided at the right of the definition and then in the illustrative phrase below it.

1. (*n.*) praise or approval; a ceremonial embrace or greeting _____

the _____ of the critics

2. (*v.*) to explain in detail _____

_____ a theory

3. (*adj.*) spotless; without blemish or fault _____

as _____ as new-fallen snow

4. (*n.*) a trite or commonplace remark; a tiresome or boring person; a sedative _____

the usual _____ served up by hack politicians

5. (*n.*) sourness or bitterness of taste; harshness or severity of manner or expression

_____

offended by the _____ of the remarks

6. (*n.*) a curse; the act of cursing

_____

hurled _____ at their enemies

7. (*adj.*) continuing over a long period of time or recurring often

_____

_____ unemployment

8. (*n.*) party strife and intrigue

_____

bitter _____ culminating in civil war

9. (*adj.*) extravagantly patriotic; blindly devoted to a cause; (*n.*) such a person

_____

a male _____

10. (*n.*) the process of wearing down by friction or gradual impairment

_____

losses due to _____

Group B

ineluctable	**stigmatize**
mercurial	**sub rosa**
palliate	**vainglory**
protocol	**vestige**
resplendent	**volition**

Pronunciation   *Match each of the words contained in Group B with its phonetic transcription. Write the appropriate word in the space given.*

1. 'vān glô rē   _____

2. vō 'lish ən   _____

3. 'prō tə kôl   _____

4. 'ves tij   _____

5. 'pal ē āt   _____

6. ri 'splen dənt   _____

7. 'stig mə tīz   _____

8. mər 'kyúr ē əl   _____

9. in i 'lək tə bəl   _____

10. səb 'rō zə   _____

Definition *Choose the word from Group B that most nearly corresponds to each of the definitions below. Write the word in the blank space provided at the right of the definition and then in the illustrative phrase below it.*

1. (*adj.*) not able to be avoided, changed, or overcome _____

    one of life's _____ facts

2. (*v.*) to brand or mark as in some way discreditable, disgraceful, or ignominious _____

    _____ by their father's misdeeds

3. (*n.*) a trace or visible evidence of something that once existed but now is lost or vanished _____

    the last _____ of an ancient civilization

4. (*adj.*) shining or gleaming brilliantly; splendid or magnificent _____

    the _____ ranks of armored knights

5. (*adj.*) characterized by rapid and unpredictable changes of mood; fickle or inconstant _____

    a(n) _____ temperament

6. (*v.*) to make less serious or severe by glossing over; to relieve without actually curing, mitigate _____

    cannot _____ the evils of autocratic rule

7. (*n.*) the power to choose, will, or decide; the act of choosing, willing, or deciding _____

    of my own _____

8. (*n.*) excessive pride in and boastfulness about one's own accomplishments or qualities; a vain show or display _____

    the _____ of a braggart

9. (*n.*) customs and regulations dealing with official behavior and etiquette, as at a court or among diplomats; a type of international agreement; a memorandum, official account or record _____

    the proper _____ in such situations

10. (*adv.*) in secret; confidentially; privately; (*adj.*) secretive _____

    given the information _____

Completing the Sentence *Choose the word for this unit that best completes each of the following sentences. Write it in the space given.*

1. His personality was so _____ that we never knew on any given occasion how he would react.

2. It was a bitter experience to have to leave the village in disgrace, followed by the jeers and _____ of people I had tried to help.

3. Have we reached the stage where anyone who refuses to go along with the majority is to be _____ as a malcontent?

4. Over the years she has tried many different remedies to relieve the pain caused by her _____ arthritis.

5. No one suggested that I take algebra in my freshman year; I decided to do it purely of my own _____ .

6. In an influential book published in 1936, the economist John M. Keynes _____ his theory of the causes of economic collapse.

7. In the innocent glow of youth and inexperience, we simply assumed that we would be able to avoid the _____ consequences of our own folly.

8. You may be scornful about matters of "mere _____ ," as you call them, but you will soon learn that *how* things are done is often as important as *what* is done.

9. The agreements that had been concluded _____ by the leaders of both parties aroused a storm of protest when they were finally made public.

10. The Founding Fathers warned that without an overriding sense of national purpose, this country could be torn apart by _____ .

11. G. B. Shaw's remark to the effect that "youth is wasted on the young" may be, as you say, an old _____ , but it is also profoundly true.

12. Many a time-honored home remedy may indeed _____ the symptoms of a disease but do little or nothing to cure it.

13. _____ in her first evening gown and her first professional hairdo, she waited impatiently for her date to escort her to the dance.

14. Isn't there truly an element of pathos in the certain knowledge that the _____ and overconfidence of our youth will be laid low by "the slings and arrows of outrageous fortune"?

15. Shall I be modest and say that I simply do not deserve these extravagant _____ , or be honest and admit that I do?

16. Since we cannot overcome the enemy by direct attack, we will wage a war of _____ against them.

17. The steady and quiet devotion of people who truly love their country is very different from the noisy fulminations of mindless _____ .

18. Why is it that so many theater critics are noted for the trenchancy of their perceptions and the _____ of their wit?

19. Despite the heat and the dirt of a summer day in the city, she managed somehow to look cool and _____ .

20. In spite of her advanced age and illness, one could still recognize the _____ of her once ravishing beauty.

Synonyms   *Choose the word for this unit that is most nearly the **same** in meaning as each of the following groups of expressions. Write it in the space given.*

1. a trace, artifact, relic; remains   _____

2. acidity, astringency, mordancy, asperity   _____

3. a cliché, platitude, commonplace   _____

4. a curse, execration, malediction   _____

5. free will; choice   _____

6. to brand, mark; to sully, taint, disgrace   _____

7. spotless, unsoiled, impeccable   _____

8. to mitigate, alleviate, extenuate   _____

9. kudos, acclaim, cheers, plaudits   _____

10. to elucidate, explicate, delineate   _____

11. a superpatriot, flag-waver, jingoist   _____

12. infighting, dissension, strife   _____

13. recurrent, persistent; inveterate, habitual   _____

14. erratic, flighty, capricious, volatile   _____

15. abrasion, erosion; exhaustion; reduction   _____

16. vanity, conceit, swaggering, pretentiousness   _____

17. secretly, covertly, stealthily, furtively   _____

18. unavoidable, inescapable, inevitable   _____

19. radiant, dazzling, splendid, glorious   _____

20. etiquette; a code of conduct; minutes   _____

Antonyms   *Choose the word for this unit that is most nearly*
*****opposite** in meaning to each of the following groups of*
expressions. Write it in the space given.

1. blandness, mellowness, mildness   _____

2. a blessing, benediction   _____

3. coercion, compulsion, duress   _____

4. boos, disapproval, censure, criticism   _____

5. avoidable, escapable, reversible, revocable   _____

6. phlegmatic, sluggish; constant, steady   _____

7. to intensify, magnify, aggravate   _____

8. dull, drab, lusterless   _____

9. humility, modesty, diffidence   _____

10. blemished, tarnished, stained, sullied   _____

11. overtly, openly   _____

12. to whitewash; to laud, extol   _____

13. unanimity, harmony, agreement, consensus   _____

14. transitory, transient, sporadic   _____

15. augmentation, proliferation, enlargement   _____

Choosing the   *Circle the **boldface** word that more satisfactorily*
Right Word   *completes each of the following sentences.*

1. His claim to be the "greatest pole-vaulter in the world" would indeed have seemed outrageously (**sub rosa, vainglorious**) if it were not for the fact that he went ahead and proved it.

2. We spent most of the evening listening to her (**palliate, expound**) her views on all sorts of interesting subjects.

3. George Washington's (**immaculate, mercurial**) reputation as a dedicated patriot has been an inspiration to many generations of Americans.

4. His talents, which had seemed so (**vestigial, resplendent**) in his youth, now struck us as unimpressive and even pathetic.

5. Beneath the (**volition, acerbity**) of their criticism, we recognized a sincere desire to help us solve our problems.

6. In the light of the lessons of history, I am skeptical about the value of any diplomatic conferences held (**sub rosa, ineluctably**).

7. They preceded her to the table, not because (**volition, protocol**) required it, but because they were eager to get at the food.

8. Letting the grim facts speak for themselves, the speaker explained quietly the (**ineluctable, resplendent**) tragedy that results from drug abuse.

9. Although she emphasizes that she was the helpless victim of bad luck, one can recognize the effects of her own (**vestige, volition**) in bringing about her downfall.

10. Although he saw himself as a wit, a bon vivant, and a man-about-town, everyone else regarded him as a hopeless (**factionalism, bromide**).

11. We are all eager to avoid the (**accolade, stigma**) of being sexist at the same time that we may be unwilling to purge ourselves of such attitudes.

12. Your threats and (**imprecations, protocols**) leave me unimpressed because I know that your words will not be followed by deeds.

13. Critics who bestow their (**stigmas, accolades**) too easily may gain some quick popularity, but they will soon lose credibility with and influence over their readers.

14. Though they are twins, one of them has a highly (**mercurial, vestigial**) temperament, while the other is stolid and reserved.

15. "My country, right or wrong" expresses (**chauvinism, attrition**) in its most common form; a more balanced view of patriotism would be: "Our country, right or wrong. When right, to keep it right; when wrong, to put it right."

16. We sought desperately for some new forms of amusement to (**palliate, stigmatize**) the boredom of those endless summer afternoons.

17. Because the difficulty of the subject matter involved increases rapidly as the term proceeds, such courses as mathematics and physics have a high rate of student (**attrition, vainglory**).

18. Our party can resist the attacks of its enemies from the outside, but it may fall victim to the erosion of (**bromide, factionalism**) from within.

19. Steve's (**chronic, resplendent**) tardiness is constantly getting him into trouble at school.

20. The small bone at the base of the spinal column in humans is thought by biologists to be the (**vestige, accolade**) of a tail.

Unit 14

Group A

accouterments	**contretemps**
apogee	**convolution**
apropos	**cull**
bicker	**disparate**
coalesce	**dogmatic**

Pronunciation   *Match each of the words contained in Group A with its phonetic transcription. Write the appropriate word in the space given.*

1. 'kon trə tän   _____

2. ə 'kü tər mənts   _____

3. dis 'par ət *or* 'dis pər it   _____

4. kon və 'lü shən   _____

5. 'ap ə jē   _____

6. 'bik ər   _____

7. kəl   _____

8. dôg 'mat ik   _____

9. ap rə 'pō   _____

10. kō ə 'les   _____

Definition   *Choose the word from Group A that most nearly corresponds to each of the definitions below. Write the word in the blank space at the right of the definition and then in the illustrative phrase below it.*

1. (*adj.*) completely distinct or different; entirely dissimilar   _____

   came from _____ backgrounds

2. (*v.*) to engage in a petty or peevish dispute; to move or run rapidly, rush; to flicker, quiver   _____

   _____ over details

3. (*n.*) the point in the orbit of a heavenly body or artificial satellite farthest from the earth; the farthest or highest point   _____

   the _____ of a long and distinguished career

4. (*n., pl.*) accessory items of clothing or equipment; a soldier's outfit, usually not including arms or clothing; trappings   _____

   the _____ of power

5. (*v.*) to pick out or select; to gather or collect _____

examples _____ from Shakespeare and the Bible

6. (*adj.*) appropriate, opportune; (*adv.*) relevantly; incidentally, by the way; speaking of _____

not really _____ to the discussion

7. (*n.*) an inopportune or embarrassing occurrence; a mishap _____

caused a(n) _____ by their blundering

8. (*adj.*) certain of the truth of one's own ideas; inclined to state opinions as if they were indisputable facts _____

a(n) _____ reply

9. (*v.*) to blend together or fuse so as to form one body or substance _____

finally _____ into a plan of action

10. (*n.*) a rolling up, coiling, or twisting together; a sinuous folding or design _____

the _____ of their logic

Group B

licentious	**probity**
mete	**repartee**
noxious	**supervene**
polemic	**truncate**
populous	**unimpeachable**

Pronunciation *Match each of the words contained in Group B with its phonetic transcription. Write the appropriate word in the space given.*

1. 'trən kāt _____

2. mēt _____

3. 'nok shəs _____

4. ən im 'pē chə bəl _____

5. rep ər 'tē _____

6. sü pər 'vēn _____

7. 'pop yə ləs _____

8. lī 'sen shəs _____

9. pə 'lem ik _____

10. 'prō bə tē _____

Definition *Choose the word from Group B that most nearly corresponds to each of the definitions below. Write the appropriate word in the blank space at the right of the definition and then in the illustrative phrase below it.*

1. (*v.*) to shorten by or as if by cutting off, lop   _____

_____ their stay

2. (*n.*) complete and confirmed honesty; total integrity   _____

questioned the _____ of their dealings

3. (*adj.*) harmful to physical health or morals   _____

overcome by _____ fumes

4. (*adj.*) beyond doubt or reproach; unquestionable   _____

a(n) _____ witness

5. (*adj.*) morally or sexually unrestrained; having no regard for accepted rules, customs, or laws   _____

their shockingly _____ behavior

6. (*n.*) an aggressive attack on or refutation of a specific opinion or doctrine   _____

deliver a(n) _____

7. (*n.*) a swift, witty reply; conversation full of such remarks; skill in making such replies or conversation   _____

sparkling _____

8. (*adj.*) full of people; filled to capacity; densely populated; having a large population   _____

the more _____ parts of the country

9. (*v.*) to take place or occur as something additional or unexpected; to follow immediately after   _____

events that _____ to blight our hopes

10. (*v.*) to distribute or apportion by or as if by measure; to allot   _____

_____ out rewards

Completing the Sentence *Choose the word for this unit that best completes each of the following sentences. Write it in the space given.*

1. I hate to _____ with you over the cost of a few gallons of gasoline, but I have to because I don't have a dime to spare.

2. Although the author's conclusions are open to debate, the scholarship upon which they are based is _____ .

3. Five minutes after arriving at the dance, I upset the punch bowl—only the first, and by no means the worst, of the innumerable _____ that made the evening a nightmare.

4. Although the premier enjoyed all the _____ of high office, in practice he was merely a figurehead who wielded very little power.

5. The lower end of the ridge had been somewhat _____ by the action of glacial erosion many thousands of years ago.

6. True, you did reply to the wisecrack, but I hardly regard "Sez you!" as an outstanding example of devastating _____ .

7. Our purpose is to help people in trouble—not to _____ out justice like a court of law.

8. It was absolutely impossible to follow the _____ of the man's tortuous reasoning as he desperately tried to prove that black was not black and white not white.

9. None of them was a fully qualified scientist, but their respective talents seemed to _____ , so that they developed into a well-rounded and highly productive research team.

10. _____ of your remarks on the probable effect of the law, may I quote from the column of a well-known political commentator?

11. Though her career in the movies had many ups and downs over the years, it reached its _____ when she won an Academy Award for best supporting actress.

12. Does "artistic freedom" justify the making of a movie that is deliberately vulgar and _____ in the hope of cashing in at the box office?

13. After the noisy excitement of the big party, the eerie silence that suddenly _____ seemed unnatural and difficult to accept.

14. Terrorist attacks on the United States are more likely to be directed at the more _____ sections of the country rather than the less populated "hinterland."

15. There are so many _____ elements in her personality and behavior that I find it difficult to tell you in any coherent way what kind of person she is and how I feel about her.

16. The report was not an impartial assessment of the problems we face; it was an intemperate _____ .

17. They possess the kind of unshakable _____ that not only precludes lying but also requires them to express the truth, no matter how painful or disadvantageous.

18. From the vast, undifferentiated mass of unsolicited manuscripts, the editor had to _____ the few that might possibly be considered for publication.

19. How can you hope to hold a fruitful conversation with people who are so _____ that they issue pronouncements instead of offering opinions?

20. How can we continue to live in this _____ atmosphere of suspicion and hatred?

Synonyms *Choose the word for this unit that is most nearly the **same** in meaning as each of the following groups of expressions. Write it in the space given.*

1. gear, equipage; trappings, appurtenances _____

2. integrity, uprightness, rectitude _____

3. a blunder, mischance, faux pas, gaffe _____

4. to squabble, wrangle, quarrel; to plash _____

5. to ensue, succeed, follow _____

6. opinionated, doctrinaire, authoritarian _____

7. wanton, dissolute, lascivious _____

8. a retort, comeback; banter, verbal sparring _____

9. to glean, choose, select, pluck _____

10. to assign, apportion, parcel out _____

11. the zenith, apex, summit, pinnacle _____

12. to amalgamate, merge, combine, unite _____

13. to trim, shorten, abbreviate, curtail _____

14. irreproachable, irrefutable, unassailable _____

15. pernicious, noisome, deleterious, toxic _____

16. pertinent, germane, apposite, relevant _____

17. crowded, teeming, swarming _____

18. dissimilar, distinct, divergent _____

19. a refutation, diatribe; a controversy _____

20. a twist, turn, complication _____

Antonyms   *Choose the word for this unit that is most nearly **opposite** in meaning to each of the following groups of expressions. Write it in the space given.*

1. questionable, debatable, dubious   _____

2. to scatter, diffuse, separate   _____

3. chaste, modest, restrained, prudish   _____

4. to precede, antecede   _____

5. to lengthen, elongate, extend, protract   _____

6. corruption, venality, immorality, iniquity   _____

7. the nadir, bottom, "pits," perigee   _____

8. to concur, agree, acquiesce   _____

9. irrelevant, inappropriate, immaterial   _____

10. wholesome, salubrious, beneficial   _____

11. similar, homogeneous, uniform   _____

12. uninhabited, unpeopled, deserted, barren   _____

13. open-minded; disinterested, dispassionate   _____

Choosing the   *Circle the **boldface** word that more satisfactorily*
Right Word   *completes each of the following sentences.*

1. When we least expected it, a crucial event (**coalesced, supervened**) that changed the entire outlook for our project.

2. Los Angeles recently supplanted Chicago as the second most (**populous, dogmatic**) city in the United States.

3. Since the original article was too long for our needs, we published it in a somewhat (**coalesced, truncated**) form.

4. We expected a simple explanation, but what we got was an involved rationalization, full of all kinds of strange (**contretemps, convolutions**).

5. I had hoped for some understanding and generosity of spirit—not this endless (**bickering, repartee**) over petty details.

6. "Unless the various factions put aside their differences and (**coalesce, supervene**) into a unified force, we will get absolutely nowhere," I said.

7. The route of the army's retreat was littered with the discarded (**polemics, accouterments**) of war.

8. I agree that she has written a very good book, but I think that it is a gross exaggeration to say that it represents the (**apogee, convolution**) of the development of the American novel.

9. What they described as a new spirit of freedom and vigorous originality seemed to me mere (**accouterments, licentiousness**).

10. In the soil prepared by ancient prejudices, economic depression, and national humiliation, there grew the (**disparate, noxious**) plants of racial and religious hatreds.

11. Even the most relentless and searching investigations by our political opponents could uncover no evidence that challenged our reputation for complete (**dogmatism, probity**).

12. I have neither the time nor the inclination to plough through those long, dreary books in the hope of (**meting, culling**) a few passages of some interest.

13. The reporter assured her boss that the charges contained in her story were based on information from a(n) (**unimpeachable, noxious**) source.

14. (**Repartee, Supervention**) has been likened to a sort of verbal fencing, with the more skillful contestants driving home their weapons for the kill.

15. If you are to get along in polite society, you must learn that a remark that is factually true is not necessarily (**populous, apropos**).

16. How do you expect to deal with the inevitable problems of life if you raise every (**repartee, contretemps**) to the level of a major tragedy?

17. Abraham Lincoln warned his countrymen that the (**convolutions, dogmas**) of the quiet past were inadequate to the needs of the stormy present.

18. We must not close our eyes to the flagrant (**disparities, contretemps**) between what our society aspires to be and what it actually is.

19. Instead of taking a fresh look at the situation and trying to find a viable solution, they were satisfied to refute their opponent by repeating old and weary (**polemics, accouterments**) of the past.

20. We are all imperfect creatures, and none of us has been divinely ordained to (**cull, mete**) out punishment to others for their transgressions.

Unit 15

Group A

adumbrate	burgeon
apotheosis	complement
ascetic	contumacious
bauble	curmudgeon
beguile	didactic

Pronunciation Match each of the words contained in Group A with its phonetic transcription. Write the appropriate word in the space given.

1. 'kom plə mənt _____

2. ə 'set ik _____

3. ə poth ē 'ō sis _____

4. kon tü 'mā shəs _____

5. 'bô bəl _____

6. 'ad əm brāt _____

7. dī 'dak tik _____

8. kər 'məj ən _____

9. bi 'gīl _____

10. 'bər jən _____

Definition Choose the word from Group A that most nearly corresponds to each of the definitions below. Write the appropriate word in the blank space at the right of the definition and then in the illustrative phrase below it.

1. (*n.*) an irascible, churlish person _____

   have a(n) _____ for a boss

2. (*v.*) to mislead or deceive; to cheat; to divert; to cause to vanish unnoticed _____

   _____ away the long afternoon

3. (*n.*) something that completes a whole; the quantity or number needed to make up a whole; the full number or allowance; (*v.*) to complete _____

   a hat to _____ her new dress

4. (*adj.*) practicing strict self-denial for the sake of personal or spiritual discipline; (*n.*) one who leads a life of self-discipline, especially to express religious devotion _____

   with the self-denial of a true _____

5. (*v.*) to outline or sketch broadly; to foreshadow or prefigure; to disclose partially

_____

_____ one's views

6. (*n.*) the elevation of a person to divine rank or status; the glorification of a person as an ideal; a glorified ideal

_____

the _____ of courage and daring

7. (*adj.*) obstinately or willfully disobedient; openly rebellious

_____

a(n) _____ attitude

8. (*v.*) to put forth new buds, leaves, or greenery; to develop rapidly or suddenly

_____

talents that suddenly _____ into maturity

9. (*n.*) a small, showy ornament of little value or use

_____

"_____ , bangles, and beads"

10. (*adj.*) intended to instruct, especially morally; inclined to moralize too much

_____

_____ poetry

Group B

disingenuous	**hauteur**
exculpate	**inhibit**
faux pas	**jeremiad**
fulminate	**opportunist**
fustian	**unconscionable**

Pronunciation   *Match each of the words contained in Group B with its phonetic transcription. Write the appropriate word in the space given.*

1. jer ə ′mī əd _____

2. ən ′kon shən ə bəl _____

3. ′ek skəl pāt _____

4. hô ′tûr _____

5. op ər ′tü nist _____

6. fō ′pä _____

7. ′ful mə nāt _____

8. ′fəs chən _____

9. dis in ′jen yü əs _____

10. in ′hib it _____

Definition   *Choose the word from Group B that most nearly corresponds to each of the definitions below. Write the appropriate word in the blank space at the right of the definition and then in the illustrative phrase below it.*

1. (*n.*) haughtiness of bearing or attitude   _____

   the studied _____ of a Russian grand duchess

2. (*n.*) an elaborate or prolonged lamentation; any tale of woe   _____

   a seemingly endless _____

3. (*adj.*) not guided or restrained by conscience, prudence, or reason; unscrupulous; immoderate   _____

   _____ behavior

4. (*n.*) a slip in manners or conduct; a social blunder   _____

   an embarrassing _____

5. (*n.*) one who makes a practice of taking advantage of circumstances to further his or her own self-interest, regardless of principles or ultimate consequences   _____

   a political _____

6. (*adj.*) lacking in sincerity or candor   _____

   a(n) _____ reply

7. (*n.*) inflated or pretentious language in speech or writing; a cloth made of cotton and flax   _____

   full of _____ and bombast

8. (*v.*) to restrain or hold back; to hinder or arrest; to prohibit   _____

   _____ one's development

9. (*v.*) to denounce or condemn vehemently; to explode, detonate   _____

   _____ against "foreign involvements"

10. (*v.*) to clear of guilt or blame   _____

   _____ by the new evidence

Completing the Sentence   *Choose the word for this unit that best completes each of the following sentences. Write it in the space given.*

1. Since there was no time to get into elaborate details, all that we did was to _____ the general features of the plan.

2. What at first appeared to be no more than a rather favorable opinion of himself has _____ into a seemingly unlimited conceit.

3. While two of the accused were indicted on conspiracy charges, the third was eventually _____ of any involvement in the plot.

4. Though your unwillingness to make me a small loan is disappointing, what infuriates me is your _____ explanation that you have made this decision "for my own good."

5. What we need in this situation is not a lugubrious _____ cataloging our troubles but a workable plan for improvements.

6. I wonder how many people have been taken in by those silly TV ads that attempt to pass off worthless _____ made of so-called "diamelles" and "faux pearls" as valuable high-grade jewelry.

7. Successful politicians must be alert to take advantage of every favorable circumstance, but if they are no more than _____ , it is hard to see how they will ever accomplish anything worthwhile.

8. In a rather silly painting called "The _____ of Homer," the artist attempts to show the blind poet's reception among the gods.

9. After his conversion, the young man renounced his former profligacy and dissipation to lead the life of a(n) _____ .

10. The chairman of the Senate Investigating Committee angrily threatened the witness with contempt charges because of her _____ attitude.

11. How could a person of your knowledge and experience allow yourself to be _____ by vague promises and empty reassurances?

12. I find it impossible to understand how the world can stand idly by while _____ acts of cruelty are daily being committed under its very nose.

13. At first, we thought that he was just pretending to be surly; but later we discovered that he really *was* an old _____ .

14. Her standards of proper behavior are so demanding that she regards every minor _____ as an unforgivable social offense.

15. For the 18th-century moralist, both art and literature had an essentially _____ purpose; they should teach as well as entertain.

16. She doesn't seem to realize that it is often more impressive to offer a few just words of criticism than to _____ long and loud against those who offend us.

17. I won't go into that shop because the snooty salespeople treat me with the _____ and disdain of an aristocrat dealing with his lackeys.

18. Instead of simply stating his case, he launched into an emotional appeal whose language soon degenerated into mere _____ and bombast.

19. We all have aggressive impulses, but in most cases our early training and conditioning tend to _____ the open expression of them.

20. The editorial argues that the crime-fighting situation cannot improve until the police department receives its full _____ of personnel.

Synonyms   *Choose the word for this unit that is most nearly the* ***same*** *in meaning as each of the following groups of expressions. Write it in the space given.*

1. a trifle, gewgaw, knickknack, bagatelle   _____

2. rant, claptrap, bombast, grandiloquence   _____

3. artful, sly, two-faced, insincere   _____

4. to delude, dupe, lure; to while away   _____

5. a balance, full allowance; to round out   _____

6. to outline, indicate; to prefigure   _____

7. austere, spartan; a celibate   _____

8. impudent, unruly, defiant, refractory   _____

9. an indiscretion, blunder, gaffe   _____

10. to absolve, exonerate, acquit   _____

11. a glorification, deification   _____

12. to restrain, repress, check, suppress   _____

13. to sprout, blossom, bloom, flourish   _____

14. to rail, denounce, inveigh   _____

15. conceit, superciliousness, snobbishness   _____

16. a grouch, crank, sorehead, churl   _____

17. a lamentation, tale of woe   _____

18. educational, instructional, moralistic   _____

19. unjustifiable, indefensible, unforgivable   _____

20. a self-seeker, exploiter   _____

Antonyms *Choose the word for this unit that is most nearly **opposite** in meaning to each of the following groups of expressions. Write it in the space given.*

1. a paean, song of praise _____

2. docile, meek, deferential, cooperative _____

3. to atrophy, wither, shrivel, diminish _____

4. to praise, applaud, commend, extol _____

5. modesty, humility, diffidence, mousiness _____

6. candid, frank, artless, sincere _____

7. to foster, promote, expedite, facilitate _____

8. a gem, precious jewel, treasure _____

9. wanton, dissolute; a hedonist _____

10. to convict, condemn, find guilty _____

11. justifiable, reasonable, honorable _____

12. a coup, tour de force _____

Choosing the Right Word *Circle the **boldface** word that more satisfactorily completes each of the following sentences.*

1. What disappointed me was not so much your failure to complete the job but your (**didactic, disingenuous**) efforts to avoid all responsibility for the debacle.

2. In a democracy, unlike a dictatorship, we have no need to disguise the human failings of our leaders; we can respect them without (**beguiling, apotheosizing**) them.

3. Having formed an opinion of you as a rather staid and conventional person, I was surprised by your (**ascetic, uninhibited**) behavior at the party.

4. They make an excellent team of leaders because his charm and deftness in handling people effectively (**complement, adumbrate**) her remarkable executive abilities.

5. In the opinion of many historians, those apparently minor incidents (**adumbrated, fulminated**) the great revolutionary uprising that was to occur only a few years later.

6. When you know that you have been guilty of rude and inconsiderate conduct, don't try to minimize your guilt by referring to the incident as a mere (**jeremiad, faux pas**).

7. The candidate underrates the electorate if she thinks she can win votes with that kind of antiquated (**curmudgeon, fustian**).

8. Unlike the Athenians, who delighted in luxury, the Spartans espoused the virtue of (**ascetic, fustian**) simplicity.

9. You have written a(n) (**didactic, unconscionable**) play with a wealth of authentic documentation, but you have overlooked the minor detail of entertaining your audience.

10. I must say that I agree with their (**inhibitions, fulminations**) against those who deface our public buildings with unsightly graffiti.

11. The author found it ironic that the play he had tossed off in his youth as a mere (**bauble, complement**) came to be viewed as his masterpiece.

12. (**Beguiled, Complemented**) by high-pressure sales talk, I bought a car that I did not need, could not afford, and did not even know how to drive.

13. The speaker referred scornfully to the "hysterical (**jeremiads, hauteurs**) of the ecologists," but I believe that they are warning us of real dangers that threaten our civilization.

14. When I asked him if he could dance, he looked at me with supreme (**disingenuousness, hauteur**) and said, "Can Pavarotti sing?"

15. You are too young to understand how the passage of the years and the trials of life can transform a happy-go-lucky youth into a solitary (**fustian, curmudgeon**).

16. The aim of the new biography was to (**exculpate, inhibit**) its subject of charges that previous biographers had wrongfully pressed against him.

17. Even the innate talents of a Mozart or an Einstein cannot (**fulminate, burgeon**) unless the environment is favorable to their growth.

18. The tactics you used to achieve your ends were not just (**opportunism, apotheosis**); they were a ruthless disregard of the rights and interests of other people.

19. What is the basis for your statement that advertising costs account for a(n) (**ascetic, unconscionable**) part of the retail price of many consumer products?

20. The situation was rapidly becoming intolerable because the new supervisor found some of the employees to be not merely uncooperative but positively (**contumacious, didactic**).

Analogies   *In each of the following, choose the item that best completes the comparison.*

1. vestigial is to **trace** as
a. rudimentary is to beginning
b. inchoate is to conclusion
c. prehensile is to grasp
d. consummate is to embryo

2. contretemps is to **embarrass** as
a. carte blanche is to inhibit
b. faux pas is to enthuse
c. quandary is to baffle
d. accolade is to constrain

3. braggart is to **vainglory** as
a. turncoat is to fidelity
b. showoff is to ostentation
c. opportunist is to volition
d. spoilsport is to factionalism

4. apotheosize is to **god** as
a. lionize is to villain
b. personify is to celebrity
c. villify is to hero
d. ostracize is to pariah

5. didactic is to **teach** as
a. monitory is to warn
b. monetary is to profit
c. mandatory is to amuse
d. minatory is to encourage

6. mercurial is to **quicksilver** as
a. contumacious is to oil
b. saccharine is to flour
c. acerbic is to sugar
d. phlegmatic is to molasses

7. immaculate is to **blemish** as
a. imperfect is to flaw
b. impeccable is to fault
c. imperative is to spot
d. impassive is to taint

8. unimpeachable is to **question** as
a. inviolable is to revere
b. unconscionable is to perform
c. ineluctable is to avoid
d. incalculable is to enjoy

9. repartee is to **scintillating** as
a. fustian is to restrained
b. bickering is to petty
c. bromide is to novel
d. fulmination is to generous

10. jeremiad is to **dolorous** as
a. diatribe is to complimentary
b. polemic is to bellicose
c. encomium is to vituperative
d. imprecation is to licentious

Identification   *In each of the following groups, circle the word that is best defined or suggested by the introductory phrase.*

1. the usual collection of platitudes
a. bromide   b. burgeon   c. apotheosis   d. beguile

2. their greatest moment
a. acerbity   b. disingenuous   c. apogee   d. cull

3. infighting among the company's directors
a. factionalism   b. convolution   c. inhibit   d. coalesce

4. put his foot in his mouth
a. protocol   b. faux pas   c. fustian   d. jeremiad

5. "By the way . . ."
a. bauble   b. contumacious   c. apropos   d. unconscionable

6. not interested in the opinions of others
a. jeremiad   b. dogmatic   c. volition   d. sub rosa

7. round out
a. complement   b. chronic   c. fustian   d. faux pas

8. soften the impact
a. ascetic   b. expound   c. disparate   d. palliate

9. put off by their snootiness
a. populous   b. exculpate   c. mercurial   d. hauteur

10. "May you never have a moment's peace!"
a. immaculate   b. imprecation   c. resplendent   d. unimpeachable

11. squabble over trifles
a. ineluctable   b. stigmatize   c. bicker   d. licentious

12. as honest as the day is long
a. noxious   b. chauvinist   c. vestige   d. probity

13. allot rewards and punishments
a. contretemps   b. mete   c. polemic   d. supervene

14. told a story to teach a moral
a. curmudgeon   b. truncate   c. didactic   d. chauvinist

Shades of Meaning	*Read each sentence carefully. Then encircle the item that best completes the sentence below it.*

Judging by the cool embrace and the perfunctory kiss, neither party found the accolade particularly agreeable.   (2)

1. In line 2 the word **accolade** most nearly means
a. praise   b. greeting   c. cheers   d. acclaim

"Thou giv'st so long, Timon,
I fear me thou wilt give away thyself in paper shortly.   (2)
What need these feasts, pomps, and vainglories?"
(Shakespeare, *Timon of Athens*, I, 2, 243–245)

2. The best definition for the word **vainglories** in line 3 is
a. boasts   b. swaggerings   c. conceits   d. displays

Doctors were at a loss to account for the malady, which was as remarkable for its virulence as for the suddenness with which it fulminated.   (2)

3. The word **fulminated** in line 2 is used to mean
a. detonated   b. denounced   c. came on   d. railed against

"I have seen
A curious child, who dwelt upon a tract   (2)
Of inland ground, applying to his ear
the convolutions of a smooth-lipped shell,   (4)
To which, in silence hushed, his very soul
Listened intensely."   (William Wordsworth, *The Excursion*)   (6)

4. In line 4 the word **convolutions** most nearly means
a. complications   b. sounds   c. folds   d. openings

Purported to be the memoranda of a series of conspirational meetings between Jews and Freemasons, the *Protocols of the Elders of Zion* were in   (2) fact forgeries concocted by the Russian secret police.

5. The word **Protocols** in line 2 is used to mean
a. regulations   b. agreements   c. codes   d. minutes

Antonyms   *In each of the following groups, circle the item that is most nearly **opposite** in meaning to the first word in **boldface type.***

1. inhibit
a. suppress
b. desert
c. promote
d. dwell

2. ineluctable
a. tolerant
b. avoidable
c. distorted
d. fragile

3. licentious
a. aggressive
b. chaste
c. humorous
d. legal

4. unimpeachable
a. irrefutable
b. partisan
c. obligatory
d. questionable

5. mercurial
a. lovable
b. sluggish
c. disdainful
d. capricious

6. apropos
a. irrelevant
b. pertinent
c. common
d. exotic

7. truncate
a. unpack
b. elongate
c. embark
d. shorten

8. populous
a. deserted
b. teeming
c. unknown
d. urban

9. contumacious
a. refractory
b. hungry
c. ardent
d. docile

10. acerbity
a. slander
b. asperity
c. mildness
d. uncertainty

11. bicker
a. argue
b. select
c. agree
d. drive

12. burgeon
a. relieve
b. rest
c. atrophy
d. flourish

13. sub rosa
a. secretly
b. overtly
c. repeatedly
d. illegally

14. factionalism
a. bigotry
b. multiplication
c. discord
d. unanimity

15. noxious
a. deleterious
b. arrogant
c. wholesome
d. isolated

16. disingenous
a. artless
b. dissembling
c. resilient
d. resourceful

17. exculpate
a. acquire
b. bury
c. deactivate
d. convict

18. ascetic
a. austere
b. fit
c. dissolute
d. sedentary

19. immaculate
a. stained
b. restrained
c. satirical
d. impeccable

20. disparate
a. divergent
b. employable
c. similar
d. distant

Completing the Sentence   *From the following list of words, choose the one that best completes each of the sentences below. Write the word in the space provided.*

Group A

coalesce	**fustian**	**opportunist**	**volition**
beguile	**repartee**	**protocol**	**apogee**

1. He is too much of a(n) _____ to be relied upon to stay with us when the other side begins to move ahead.

2. His speeches are filled with _____ and bombast—in sharp contrast to the subdued, constructive comments of his opponent.

3. "Now that I'm at the _____ of my career," the actress said, "I guess I have nowhere to go from here but down."

R

4. No one told me to go out for the football team; I did it entirely of my own

_____ .

5. "_____ requires that I report to the Foreign Office as soon as I arrive," the diplomat observed.

Group B

bicker	ascetic	supervene	ineluctable
adumbrate	inhibit	contumacious	cull

1. The students _____ statistics from various reference works to use in their research project in economics.

2. While he resided in his little cabin beside Walden Pond, Henry Thoreau lived a life as simple and _____ as that of a monk.

3. Far from seeking to _____ political debate, a democratic society welcomes and encourages the free exchange of ideas.

4. In her opening remarks, the prosecutor briefly _____ the case that the state would bring against the defendant.

5. I think your accounting of the costs is wrong, but it is beneath my dignity to _____ with you over a few dollars.

Word Families

A. *On the line provided, write a **noun form** for each of the following words.*

EXAMPLE: supervene—**supervention**

1. stigmatize _____

2. fulminate _____

3. inhibit _____

4. mercurial _____

5. disparate _____

6. dogmatic _____

7. licentious _____

8. populous _____

9. contumacious _____

10. didactic _____

11. beguile _____

12. palliate _____

13. resplendent _____

B. *On the line provided, write an* **adjective** *related to each of the following words.*

EXAMPLE: opportunist—**opportunistic**

1. acerbity _____

2. factionalism _____

3. vainglory _____

4. vestige _____

5. polemic _____

6. inhibit _____

7. palliate _____

Filling the Blanks   *Circle the pair of words that best complete the meaning of each of the following passages.*

1. "The man is not a disinterested observer of the passing scene," I said. "He is essentially a(n) _____ who uses his column in the newspaper as a kind of soapbox from which to _____ , like some Old Testament prophet, against the iniquities of those around him."

   a. curmudgeon . . . exculpate   c. opportunist . . . truncate
   b. chauvinist . . . palliate   d. polemicist . . . fulminate

2. During the election of 1860, the Democrats could not present a united front because the party was torn asunder by _____ strife and petty regional _____ .

   a. factional . . . bickering   c. dogmatic . . . repartee
   b. contumacious . . . attrition   d. unconscionable . . . vainglory

3. During the Civil War, Robert E. Lee's freedom of choice was seriously _____ by the fact that the South could never replace the losses it sustained through normal battlefield _____ .

   a. palliated . . . volition   c. truncated . . . convolution
   b. inhibited . . . attrition   d. adumbrated . . . imprecation

4. For the 18th century, all art had two _____ purposes: "to point a moral or adorn a tale." Accordingly, no work was judged to be really complete if either the _____ or the decorative element was not in evidence.

   a. vestigial . . . dogmatic   c. complementary . . . didactic
   b. ineluctable . . . licentious   d. unimpeachable . . . chauvinistic

Analogies   *In each of the following, choose the item that best completes the comparison.*

1. repartee is to **persiflage** as
a. apogee is to nadir
b. macrocosm is to microcosm
c. probity is to rectitude
d. plethora is to dearth

2. paean is to **joy** as
a. jeremiad is to sorrow
b. aria is to despair
c. lucubration is to elation
d. polemic is to boredom

3. homily is to **didactic** as
a. corollary is to moot
b. caveat is to cautionary
c. mnemonic is to dogmatic
d. liturgy is to ancillary

4. apropos is to **apposite** as
a. ascetic is to hedonistic
b. gargantuan is to dwarfish
c. mercurial is to phlegmatic
d. lugubrious is to lachrymose

5. accolade is to **hero** as
a. melee is to vassal
b. apotheosis is to villain
c. imprecation is to saint
d. obloquy is to poltroon

6. bromide is to **banal** as
a. non sequitur is to logical
b. philippic is to acerbic
c. elixir is to ineffable
d. vignette is to ribald

7. accouterments are to **wear** as
a. accessories are to pay
b. utensils are to collect
c. durables are to read
d. comestibles are to eat

8. patrician is to **hauteur** as
a. lackey is to independence
b. curmudgeon is to amiability
c. sycophant is to servility
d. mountebank is to prescience

9. resplendent is to **shine** as
a. effusive is to gush
b. vestigial is to flow
c. sanguine is to trickle
d. abortive is to cascade

10. noxious is to **harm** as
a. portentous is to wealth
b. salubrious is to health
c. bilious is to pleasure
d. traumatic is to ease

Shades of Meaning   *Read each sentence carefully. Then encircle the item that best completes the sentence below it.*

A consequence of the Creek War of 1813–1814 was the deracination of the defeated Creek Indians and their forcible relocation to what is now Oklahoma.   (2)

1. In line 1 the word **deracination** is used to mean
a. elimination   b. uprooting   c. eradication   d. surrender

"Where's the cook? Is supper ready, the house trimmed, rushes strewed, cobwebs swept, the serving men in their new fustian, the white stockings, and every officer his wedding garment on?"   (2)
(Shakespeare, *The Taming of The Shrew,* IV, 1, 40–43)

2. The word **fustian** in line 2 most nearly means
a. pretentious writing   c. claptrap
b. inflated speech   d. uniform

So that the medicine goes down "in the most delightful way," children's painkillers usually consist of an analgesic suspended in an elixir.   (2)

3. The best definition for the word **elixir** in line 2 is
a. panacea   b. tonic   c. sweet liquid   d. potion

Until recent times it was the custom for gentlemen to dress in formal wear—
including claque and gloves—when attending the opera. **(2)**

4. The word **claque** in line 2 is used to mean
   a. hangers-on   b. fan club   c. flatterers   d. hat

"In bosky shade of highland glen
where dappled sunbeams fling and flicker **(2)**
A bonny brook by sylvan sprites is ken
To tumble, traipse, and bravely bicker." **(4)**
      (A.E. Glug, "Forth to the Firth," IV, 103–106)

5. In line 4 the word **bicker** most nearly means
   a. plash   b. wrangle   c. quarrel   d. quiver

**Filling
the Blanks**
*Encircle the pair of words that best complete each of
the following passages.*

1. Since the man has repeatedly shown himself to be nothing more than a

self-seeking _____ who will not scruple to achieve his aims

by whatever means are at hand, I feel we have every right in the world to

question the _____ of his dealings in the present situation.

   a. opportunist . . . probity   c. curmudgeon . . . acerbity
   b. chauvinist . . . hauteur   d. ascetic . . . protocol

2. The eventual _____ of a decidedly unsightly larva into a(n)

_____ colored monarch or swallowtail butterfly is surely one

of the most awesome wonders of nature.

   a. vagary . . . effusively   c. metamorphosis . . . flamboyantly
   b. acumen . . . fulsomely   d. euphoria . . . zanily

3. I began to understand how profoundly John F. Kennedy's assassination

had _____ his wife, Jacqueline, when I noticed that she

seemed to perform her part in her husband's _____ as if

she were sleepwalking.

   a. modulated . . . divination   c. browbeaten . . . emolument
   b. traumatized . . . obsequies   d. immured . . . homily

4. The verve and _____ with which the leading lady played

her part did a great deal to make up for the _____ and

indifferent performances turned in by the rest of the cast.

   a. casuistry . . . prolix   c. bathos . . . inchoate
   b. empathy . . . fervid   d. élan . . . lackluster

5. Though George Frederick Handel envisaged *Solomon* more as a pageant

than as a(n) _____ , the underlying didactic purpose of the

work is revealed in the deep sense of spirituality with which the composer

_____ the music.

   a. homily . . . imbued   c. polemic . . . truncated
   b. bromide . . . palliated   d. aberration . . . inhibited

Final Mastery Test

I. Selecting Word Meanings
*In each of the following groups, circle the word or expression that is most nearly **the same** in meaning as the word in **boldface type** in the introductory phrase.*

1. a **harbinger** of happier days
a. guarantee
b. herald
c. memory
d. enjoyment

2. remaining **immaculate** in all circumstances
a. calm
b. indifferent
c. spotless
d. sagacious

3. a group torn apart by **factionalism**
a. quarrels over money
b. lack of communication
c. wild emotionalism
d. partisan differences

4. players who **complemented** each other's abilities
a. nullified
b. reinforced and completed
c. praised
d. mocked

5. the **depredations** of the invaders
a. victories
b. defeats
c. strategic plans
d. plunder and destruction

6. **adumbrated** the problems facing us
a. overcame
b. avoided
c. outlined
d. pondered

7. whose forces were diminished by **attrition**
a. unnecessary expenditures
b. gradual wearing away
c. natural disasters
d. flagrant inefficiency

8. will not accept such **unconscionable** delays
a. severely damaging
b. repeated many times
c. utterly unjustified
d. motivated by malice

9. an **inchoate** instrument of government
a. lacking high ideals
b. in an early stage of development
c. corrupt
d. bureaucratic

10. took pleasure in pointing out the **solecisms** in my essay
a. violations of rules
b. puns and jokes
c. changing standards
d. new ideas

11. could not fail to recognize her **mellifluous** voice
a. rasping
b. smooth and sweet
c. shrill
d. obviously affected

12. a **morass** of doubts and misunderstandings
a. swamp
b. comedy
c. scholarly analysis
d. collection

13. showed great **prescience** in formulating policies
a. courage
b. determination
c. human sympathy
d. foresight

14. wounded in the **melee**
a. trap
b. fight
c. arm
d. crisis

15. not particularly amused by his attempts at **persiflage**
a. good-natured banter
b. impersonation
c. mime
d. bitter satire

16. the **jeremiads** of the old preacher
a. brilliant oratory
b. prolonged lamentations
c. sincere appeals
d. anecdotes

17. a **lugubrious** expression on his face
a. mournful
b. optimistic
c. determined
d. panic-stricken

18. critical of their **supine** attitude
a. marked by self-interest
b. superior
c. passive and submissive
d. aggressively uncooperative

19. in the **lexicon** of youth
a. set of values
b. vocabulary
c. time frame
d. inexperience

20. is constantly being misled by **mirages**
a. illusions
b. criminal acts
c. faulty instructions
d. inadequate preparation

21. singularly **maladroit** in making the arrangements
a. lacking finesse and skill
b. accomplished
c. considerate of others
d. wasteful

22. annoyed by their **niggardly** methods
a. finicky
b. stingy
c. dishonest
d. insulting

23. the **noisome** stereotypes of racial bigotry
a. foul and offensive
b. expressed in a loud voice
c. perpetuated
d. misleading

24. willing to overlook our **peccadilloes**
a. minor faults
b. lack of faith
c. blatant dishonesty
d. poor taste

25. a **schism** in the ranks of the political party
a. infusion of new strength
b. spread of corruption
c. split
d. mass confusion

26. some leeway for interpretation within the **parameters** of the style
a. incidental difficulties
b. determining elements
c. unknown quantities
d. revolutionary ideas

27. hit upon an answer after long **lucubration**
a. delay
b. silence
c. experimentation
d. thought

28. furniture selected purely for **utilitarian** purposes
a. aesthetic
b. practical
c. sentimental
d. economical

29. discovered that mathematics was her **forte**
a. weakness
b. consuming interest
c. strong point
d. nemesis

30. a **disingenuous** reply
a. lacking in frankness
b. exceptionally creative
c. devoid of human feelings
d. genial and warmhearted

FMT

II. Words That Describe People

Some words that are used to describe people are listed below. In the space before each word in Column A, write the letter of the corresponding brief description in Column B.

Column A

_____ 31. **waggish**

_____ 32. **ascetic**

_____ 33. **curmudgeon**

_____ 34. **fastidious**

_____ 35. **poltroon**

_____ 36. **mercurial**

_____ 37. **philistine**

_____ 38. **mountebank**

_____ 39. **insouciant**

_____ 40. **narcissistic**

Column B

a. much concerned with details and niceties

b. a trickster or phony

c. practicing strict self-denial

d. stuck on oneself

e. scornful of artistic values or the "finer things of life"

f. showing contemptible cowardice

g. a surly and cantankerous person

h. given to making jokes

i. inclined to make oneself conspicuous and "important"

j. carefree; not disposed to worry about dangers or consequences

k. showing rapid changes in temperament and attitude

III. Words Connected with Occupations

The words in Column A are associated with professions and other occupations. In the space before each word, write the letter of the item in Column B that best identifies it.

Column A

_____ 41. **therapeutic**

_____ 42. **protocol**

_____ 43. **virtuoso**

_____ 44. **divination**

_____ 45. **homily**

_____ 46. **adjudicate**

_____ 47. **lachrymose**

_____ 48. **bowdlerize**

_____ 49. **persona**

_____ 50. **lampoon**

Column B

a. satirical writers

b. fortune-tellers

c. mediators between quarreling groups

d. writers of sentimental tragedies

e. workers in precious metals

f. members of the clergy

g. diplomats

h. doctors and nurses

i. concert violinists

j. actors and actresses

k. editors who seek to make classics "more suitable" for young readers

146

IV. Word Pairs

In the space before each of the following pairs of words write:

S — if the words are synonyms or near-synonyms.
O — if the words are antonyms or near-antonyms.
N — if the words are not directly related in meaning.

_____ **51.** disparate—identical   _____ **59.** hidebound—stodgy

_____ **52.** bibulous—bilious   _____ **60.** pundit—malcontent

_____ **53.** plebeian—patrician   _____ **61.** microcosm—macrocosm

_____ **54.** obloquy—acclaim   _____ **62.** minuscule—gargantuan

_____ **55.** coalesce—amalgamate   _____ **63.** liaison—protégé

_____ **56.** symptomatic—malleable   _____ **64.** lackluster—drab

_____ **57.** quixotic—practicable   _____ **65.** cozen—inveigle

_____ **58.** wanton—licentious

V. Foreign Words and Phrases

Listed below are some words and phrases commonly used in present-day English that are taken directly from foreign languages. The sentences following suggest the meanings of these expressions. Write the appropriate word or phrase on the line next to each sentence.

fait accompli	sic	mot juste	carte blanche
non sequitur	volte-face	cul-de-sac	ad hoc
sub rosa	hoi polloi	de facto	quid pro quo

66. The treaty negotiations will be successful only if each of the parties makes concessions to the other, so that both can feel they are obtaining fair compensation.

_____

67. I was shocked when he abandoned the cause he had backed so long and became an advocate of a diametrically opposed program.

_____

68. When they returned home and found the business completely reorganized and functioning successfully, they simply had to accept the new situation.

_____

69. By my lies and deceptions, I had maneuvered myself into an impossible position from which I could neither advance nor retreat.

_____

70. It is foolish of you to conclude that she is an expert in "Oriental psychology" just because she made a two-week tour of the Far East.

_____

71. When Fran referred to him as an "intellectual snob," I felt that she had found the perfect epithet on which to skewer his pretentious personality.

_____

FMT

72. The committee has been set up to conduct the investigation, and it will pass out of existence as soon as its job is completed.

_____

73. The truth is that racial segregation still exists in some parts of the United States, even though it is not sanctioned by law.

_____

74. When Mrs. Roth put Larry in charge of the class play, she gave him full authority to select the cast, prepare the sets, and make all other major decisions.

_____

75. The author added a word to indicate that the misuse of "disinterested" for "uninterested" actually appeared in the book he was quoting.

_____

VI. Word Associations

In each of the following, circle the expression that best completes the meaning of the sentence or answers the question, with particular relation to the meaning of the word in **boldface type**.

76. If you refer to someone's reactions as **maudlin,** you are
   a. expressing sympathy
   b. complaining of excessive sentimentality
   c. showing utter indifference
   d. charging deliberate misrepresentation

77. Which of the following might properly be described as a **faux pas**?
   a. scoring the winning touchdown
   b. attending a formal party in blue jeans
   c. eating a hearty breakfast
   d. learning to water-ski

78. Which of the following indicates **kudos**?
   a. "Get out of my life!"
   b. "Do what I say, not what I do."
   c. "What have I done to deserve this?"
   d. "You're the greatest!"

79. The **vicissitudes** of life refers to its
   a. beginning and end
   b. ups and downs
   c. pleasures
   d. side issues

80. What advice might you give to a person who is guilty of a **tautology**?
   a. "See your doctor immediately."
   b. "Don't repeat yourself."
   c. "Stop that abusive language."
   d. "Speak more slowly and distinctly."

81. Which of the following would be most likely to accept a philosophy of **nihilism**?
   a. a deeply religious person
   b. an accomplished physicist
   c. a conservative
   d. a sweeping critic of the social order

82. What is the prevailing mood of a speaker who delivers a **philippic**?
   a. smug self-satisfaction
   b. joyful approbation
   c. bitter disapproval
   d. impartiality

83. Which of the following is typical of **nepotism**?
   a. giving good jobs to relatives
   b. donating large sums to charity
   c. advancing the public interest
   d. suffering delusions of persecution

84. We would expect **aficionados** of the opera to
   a. picket the local opera house
   b. attend opera performances often
   c. sing the lead roles in _Carmen_
   d. never go to an opera

85. A person who may properly be described as an **opportunist** is trying hard to
a. help others
b. get ahead at any cost
c. maintain law and order
d. stay young and beautiful

86. What would be the most logical thing to do if you were in a **labyrinth**?
a. sit down and enjoy the show
b. deliver a eulogy to the departed
c. start the motor and drive off
d. try to find your way out

87. Your situation might well be described as **precarious** if you were
a. lolling in a hammock
b. hanging from the edge of a cliff
c. playing tennis with a weak opponent
d. attending the Senior Prom

88. An editorial writer who refers to a strike as **internecine** believes that
a. the strike will be successful
b. all parties involved will suffer greatly
c. labor is justified in calling the strike
d. the strike will end soon

89. People who are affected by **xenophobia** are
a. fond of rich foods
b. afraid of heights
c. suspicious of foreigners
d. unlucky in love

90. Deeds of **derring-do** are associated particularly with
a. knights-errant
b. politicians
c. suburban commuters
d. scholars and intellectuals

91. Which of the following might you seek to **deracinate**?
a. fun and games
b. old friends and good companions
c. tree stumps and bad habits
d. patience and fortitude

92. To say that a person is **bickering** over the terms of a contract implies
a. praise for being careful
b. disapproval of the contract provisions
c. complete indifference
d. criticism for being petty

93. People who indulge in **casuistry** are most likely
a. overeating
b. spreading rumors
c. splitting hairs
d. feeling sorry for themselves

94. An **empirical** analysis of a problem is based primarily on
a. the laws of chance
b. preconceived ideas
c. wishful thinking
d. experience

95. A person who has just received a **lagniappe** would most likely
a. take some medication
b. say "Thanks!"
c. seek revenge
d. mend his or her ways

96. Which of the following expresses the attitude of a **dogmatic** person?
a. "I may be wrong."
b. "I'm waiting for more evidence."
c. "What do you think about it?"
d. "I'm right, and that's that!"

97. Which of the following best describes the mood and atmosphere of a **gothic** novel?
a. bright and cheerful
b. dark and gloomy
c. zany and slapstick
d. sophisticated and satirical

98. A **flamboyant** personality suggests a
a. demure little wren
b. bold eagle
c. perky robin
d. showy peacock

99. From a renowned **raconteur** you would expect
a. a superb dinner
b. an entertaining story
c. expert legal advice
d. the perfect crime

100. You would be likely to regard it as a **contretemps** if you
a. improved your vocabulary
b. won first prize in an essay contest
c. helped your classmates
d. did poorly on this Final Mastery Test

Building with Word Roots

Units 1–3

sem, simil, simul—like; together, at the same time

This root appears in **verisimilitude** (page 13), which means "the appearance of being true." Some other words based on the same root are listed below.

assemblage	**disassemble**	**simile**	**simulation**
assimilation	**resemblance**	**simulacrum**	**simulcast**

From the list of words above, choose the one that best corresponds to each of the brief definitions below. Write the word in the space at the right of the definition, and then in the illustrative phrase below the definition.

1. to take apart   _____

_____ the set

2. the act or process of taking on the appearance or form of something; a feigning or pretending   _____

a convincing _____ of surprise

3. a comparison, introduced by *like* or *as*; an analogy   _____

a poetic use of _____

4. to broadcast over radio and television at the same time   _____

turn on the _____ of the rock concert

5. the act or process of taking in or absorbing; the state of being absorbed   _____

the _____ of knowledge

6. a collection of people or things; a gathering   _____

a(n) _____ of notables

7. an image or representation of something; an unreal or superficial semblance   _____

a(n) _____ of happiness

8. a similarity in form or appearance; a likeness   _____

bore a family _____

From the list of words above, choose the one that best completes each of the following sentences. Write the word in the space provided.

1. The mechanic was forced to _____ the entire transmission in order to replace the faulty part.

2. Members of the police emergency negotiating team rehearse their demanding roles in lifelike _____ of hostage situations.

3. French purists have gone to great lengths to resist any further_____ of English words and phrases into their language.

4. Though they were not related by blood, the _____ between them was so stong that many took them for twins.

5. Displayed in Madame Tussaud's museum in London are _____ fashioned in wax of historical personages and notorious criminals.

6. It was a matchless _____ of politicians and philosophers who gathered in Philadelphia in 1787 to frame our Constitution.

7. We watched the _____ of Puccini's *La Boheme* on television while listening to it on our local public radio station.

8. The instructor warned his creative-writing students against using such timeworn

_____ as "red as a rose" and "blue as the sky."

Units 4–6

gen—race, kind, class; origin, birth

This root appears in **genre** (page 38), which means "a type, class, or variety, especially with relation to literary composition or painting." Some other words based on the same root are listed below.

carcinogen	**degenerate**	**generic**	**genocide**
congenital	**genealogy**	**genesis**	**homogeneous**

From the list of words above, choose the one that best corresponds to each of the brief definitions below. Write the word in the space at the right of the definition, and then in the illustrative phrase below the definition.

1. existing at birth; constituting an essential characteristic as if by birth, inherent _____

a _____ liar

2. relating to an entire group or class; not protected by trademark, nonproprietary _____

_____ names

3. a record or account of a family's or a person's descent; lineage; the study of ancestry and family histories _____

traced her _____

4. to deteriorate or decline physically or morally; exhibiting such decline; a morally degraded person _____

condemned their _____ behavior

5. the systematic extermination of a racial, political, or cultural group

_____

_____ of unprecedented proportions

6. creation, origin; the coming into being of something

_____

the _____ of the idea

7. a cancer-causing substance

_____

tested the additive for _____

8. uniform in composition; like in nature or kind

_____

a _____ group of students

From the list of words on page 150, choose the one that best completes each of the following sentences. Write the word in the space provided.

1. Tribal leaders branded the regime's plan to "relocate" the remaining native population as tantamount to _____ .

2. When I stumbled across an old family _____ , I discovered that I am descended from a veteran of the Revolutionary War.

3. Rather than specify a particular brand, many doctors now prescribe less expensive _____ drugs for their patients.

4. Consumer groups petitioned the government to ban the pesticide when it was discovered to contain a proven _____ .

5. The _____ of Herman Melville's masterpiece _Moby Dick_ lay in the author's experiences as a seaman aboard a whaling vessel.

6. The debate, which had begun as a high-minded and civil exchange of views, rapidly _____ into an ugly, name-calling brawl.

7. The argument boiled down to a dispute over how much of one's character is _____ and how much is acquired.

8. The designers had carefully coordinated the wallpaper, upholstery, and drapery to lend the room a _____ appearance.

Unit 7–9

mal—bad, ill

This root appears in **malcontent** (page 67), which means "one who is dissatisfied with conditions." Some other words based on the same root are listed below.

maladapted	**malfeasance**	**malfunction**	**malingerer**
malaise	**malformation**	**malice**	**malodorous**

From the list of words on page 151, choose the one that best corresponds to each of the brief definitions below. Write the word in the space at the right of the definition, and then in the illustrative phrase below the definition.

1. a desire to cause harm or suffering; deep-seated ill will _____

_____ aforethought

2. one who pretends to be ill in order to escape duty or work _____

a shiftless _____

3. having a bad odor; ill-smelling; highly improper _____

_____ cheeses

4. wrongdoing or misconduct in public office _____

accused of _____

5. unsuited or poorly suited for a particular purpose or situation _____

_____ for use as a classroom

6. a vague feeling of physical or mental discomfort _____

overcome by _____

7. a failure to operate correctly or in a normal manner; to operate poorly or imperfectly _____

a technical _____

8. an abnormal or faulty bodily structure or part _____

an unsightly _____

From the list of words on page 151, choose the one that best completes each of the following sentences. Write the word in the space provided.

1. The review panel found the department head guilty of _____ in handling the funds for public housing.

2. Lincoln believed that national unity could never be restored if the South were treated with _____ rather than magnanimity.

3. A _____ vapor seemed to waft from the fetid bog.

4. Advances in reconstructive surgery have permitted doctors to correct many _____ that once would have been untreatable.

5. The _____ of a simple switching device set off a chain reaction that culminated in a complete power failure.

6. The woman's delicate constitution and refined sensibility were _____ to the rough-and-tumble life of the frontier.

7. The new captain personally visited the ship's sickbay to make sure that no _____ were being harbored there.

8. Who has not suffered that indefinable sense of _____ that so often accompanies the onset of the flu?

Units 10–12

chron—time

This Greek root appears in **anachronism** (page 87), which means "a misplacing in time of persons, events, or customs in regard to each other." Some other words based on the same root are listed below.

chronically	**chronicler**	**chronology**	**crony**
chronicle	**chronological**	**chronometer**	**cronyism**

From the list of words above, choose the one that best corresponds to each of the brief definitions below. Write the word in the space at the right of the definition, and then in the illustrative phrase below the definition.

1. an exceptionally accurate clock, watch, or other timepiece   _____

     an underwater _____

2. the determination of dates or of the sequence of events; the sequential ordering of dates or events; such a list or table   _____

     a _____ of key battles

3. constantly, habitually, over a prolonged period   _____

     _____ late

4. arranged in order of time or occurrence; relating to or in keeping with the ordering of events in time   _____

     a _____ listing of the composer's works

5. a close friend or companion, chum   _____

     a reunion of old school _____

6. a record of historical events presented in order of occurrence; to make or keep such a record   _____

     _____ the empire's rise and fall

7. favoritism shown to old friends or companions in official or political appointments   _____

     accused the dean of _____

8. one who writes or keeps a record of historical events   _____

     a _____ of fashion

From the list of words on page 153, choose the one that best completes each of the following sentences. Write the word in the space provided.

1. Historians like Tacitus and Gibbon do not merely _____ events, but interpret their meaning and importance as well.

2. Hopelessly poor and _____ ill, the wretched man despaired of ever finding relief from his incessant suffering.

3. The _____ was guaranteed not to deviate more than five seconds from the correct time over the course of a year.

4. Police detectives drew up a _____ to show in proper sequence the events leading up to the crime.

5. When the governor began to fill key administration posts with his old business pals, the press accused him of _____ .

6. Students were given a list of important events in American History and asked to arrange them in correct _____ order.

7. A Benedictine monk, whom we now call the Venerable Bede, was an important _____ of Christianity's growth in Anglo-Saxon England.

8. The retired Senator liked nothing more than to swap stories with a group of old _____ .

Units 13–15

temp—time

This Latin root appears in **contretemps** (page 122), which means "an inopportune or embarrassing mishap." Some other words based on the same root are listed below.

contemplative	**ex tempore**	**temperance**	**tempest**
contemporaneous	**temperamentally**	**temperature**	**tempestuous**

From the list of words above, choose the one that best corresponds to each of the brief definitions below. Write the word in the space at the right of the definition, and then in the illustrative phrase below the definition.

1. by nature or disposition; moodily; impulsively _____

_____ unsuited for the job

2. a violent storm; a tumult, uproar _____

floundered in the raging _____

3. in an impromptu, unrehearsed manner; on the spur of the moment _____

delivered the speech _____

4. existing or occurring at the same period of time   _____

    _____ with Shakespeare

5. moderation, self-restraint; total abstinence from alcohol   _____

    preached _____ in all things

6. the degree of hotness or coldness in a body or an
environment; the specific degree of hotness or coldness
as measured on a scale   _____

    running a _____

7. stormy; violent; turbulent   _____

    a _____ relationship

8. inclined to consider intently, thoughtful; meditative;
pensive   _____

    a(n) _____ pose

---

*From the list of words on page 154, choose the one that best
completes each of the following sentences. Write the word in
the space provided.*

1. The Restoration Period in England was roughly _____ with the
beginning of the reign of Louis XIV in France.

2. You may regard the controversy as one of far-reaching importance, but in my
opinion it is merely a(n) _____ in a teacup.

3. When we learned that we were competing for the final spot on the roster,
the _____ of our friendship began to cool noticeably.

4. Her hatchet raids on saloons made Carrie Nation one of the most celebrated
crusaders of the _____ movement.

5. After the _____ events of the French Revolution and
Napoleonic Wars, Europe settled down to an era of relative peace and quiet.

6. In his "Portrait of a Woman Deep in Thought," the painter has magically captured
his subject's _____ mood.

7. Her memorial tribute to the departed was all the more moving because it was
delivered _____ rather than from prepared notes.

8. Shakespeare portrays Richard II as more a poet than a prince, and on that account
_____ unfit to rule England.

Enhancing Your Vocabulary

Units 1–3

Eponyms   A good many English words derive from the names of the people who were originally associated with the object, practice, or attitude that the word indicates. Such words are called *eponyms*. A good example of an eponym is **bowdlerize**, introduced on page 19. This word, as you probably already know, comes from the name of the 19th century English editor who published a 10-volume edition of the works of William Shakespeare in which "those words [were] omitted which [could not] with propriety be read aloud in a family." A number of other useful eponyms are listed below.

boycott   **quisling**
gerrymandering   **sandwich**
lynch   **shrapnel**
maverick

From the list of words given above, choose the item that corresponds to each of the following brief definitions. Write the word in the blank provided.

1. a traitor, turncoat, or collaborator with an enemy   _____

Person Involved: the Norwegian politician who helped the Nazis invade and take over his native country during World War II

2. a fragment from a bomb, mine, or shell   _____

Person Involved: the British artillery officer who invented an early type of fragmentation bomb

3. to execute illegally, usually by hanging   _____

Person Involved: the Virginia justice of the peace who suppressed Tory (Loyalist) activities during the American Revolution by this method

4. a nonconformist or dissenter   _____

Person Involved: the Texas cattleman who went against accepted practice by refusing to brand his calves

5. the practice of dividing an area into oddly shaped electoral districts to give one party unfair advantage during an election   _____

Person Involved: the Governor of Massachusetts who created such an election district in 1812

6. Two slices of bread with meat or other filling between them _____

Person Involved: the British diplomat who, reluctant to stop gambling to eat a meal, had his chef invent something that could be eaten without cutlery

7. to refuse to buy, use, or deal with as a way to protest, or force the acceptance of, some form of behavior; a protest _____

Person Involved: the land agent in County Mayo, Ireland, who was subjected to such treatment in 1880 when he refused to lower rents on the lands he managed

From the list of words on page 156, choose the item that best completes each of the following sentences. Write the word in the space provided.

1. During the civil rights movement of the 1950's and 1960's, both blacks and whites

   _____ segregated lunch counters, bus depots, and schools.

2. Though I always have a full meal at dinnertime, I never have much more than a(n)

   _____ for lunch.

3. When the bomb exploded in our midst, two soldiers were killed outright, and three

   were wounded by _____ .

4. Many a western from the 1940's and 1950's contains a scene in which an angry

   crowd, intent upon _____ a prisoner in the sheriff's custody,
   gathers outside the local pokey.

5. The city was finally taken when, late one night, a few _____
   overpowered the guards and opened the gates to the enemy.

6. The man is considered something of a(n)_____ in political circles
   because he tends to march to a different drummer from the rest of the legislature.

7. In 1965, Congress passed a law designed to end _____ and
   equalize populations in Congressional districts.

Units 4–6

**Words
from
Unusual
Sources**

The inclusion of **pundit** in Unit 4 brings to mind the fact that present-day English contains a good many words derived from striking or unusual sources. *Pundit* (page 32), for example, comes from Hindi, one of the languages of India. Listed below are a number of other "exotic" items in our vocabulary.

amok (amuck)	**mumbo jumbo**
caucus	**taboo**
kowtow	**tycoon**
mufti	

From the list of expressions given above, choose the item that corresponds to each of the brief definitions below. Write the expression in the space provided.

1. an expression of respect or submission; to show servile
   deference to   _____

   Source: Chinese

2. in a frenzy of violence and killing; in a blind, undisciplined,
   or faulty manner   _____

   Source: Malay

3. a wealthy, powerful, and highly successful businessman or
   woman   _____

   Source: Japanese, but ultimately from Chinese

4. a closed meeting of the members of a political party called to decide questions of policy or choose candidates _____

   Source: North American Indian (Algonquian)

5. civilian dress, especially when worn by someone who usually wears a uniform _____

   Source: Arabic

6. a prohibition excluding something from use or mention; forbidden _____

   Source: Polynesian (Tongan)

7. unintelligible or incomprehensible language; complicated, obscure, and seemingly purposeless activity _____

   Source: African (Mandingo)

From the list of expressions on page 157, choose the item that completes each of the following sentences. Write it in the space provided.

1. When my boss turned up at the office in an old sweat shirt and jeans, instead of his usual 3-piece suit, I said, "How nice to see you in _____ for a change!"

2. Suddenly one of the elephants ran _____ and trampled some of the people in the crowd.

3. At first, Presidential candidates were chosen by party _____ operating mainly in the state legislatures.

4. I have absolutely no intention of _____ to that arrogant lout just because he's a mighty senior and I'm a lowly freshman.

5. Though she started out with hardly a dime to her name, she became one of the most successful _____ in the industry.

6. I sometimes find all the _____ involved in running for high political office in this country a bit ridiculous.

7. Many of the _____ that inhibited social intercourse during the Victorian era have been relaxed or discarded in the 20th century.

Units 7–9

Loanwords from Greek

Even though you have probably never studied Greek, you may actually know some. That is because English has borrowed quite a few Greek words and phrases with little or no change (allowing, of course, for the difference in alphabets). One such expression is **kudos,** introduced on page 74. Some others are listed below.

aroma	**pathos**
catharsis	**phenomenon**
climax	**psyche**
hubris	

EYV

From the words listed on page 158, choose the item that corresponds to each of the brief definitions below. Write the word in the space provided.

1. the quality of arousing pity or compassion; a feeling of pity, sympathy, or tenderness _____

    Original Greek Meaning: "suffering, emotion"

2. a pleasant odor that is characteristic of something _____

    Original Greek Meaning: "spice"

3. any occurrence or fact perceptible to the senses; a marvel; a paragon _____

    Original Greek Meaning: "that which appears"

4. the point of greatest intensity in a series of events; to reach or bring about such a point _____

    Original Greek Meaning: "ladder"

5. excessive pride, arrogance, or self-confidence _____

    Original Greek Meaning: "insolence, outrage"

6. the soul or spirit; the mind _____

    Original Greek Meaning: "breath, life, soul"

7. a purification or purging; a figurative release of tension or the emotions _____

    Original Greek Meaning: "purging"

From the list of words given on page 158, choose the item that best completes each of the following sentences. Write it in the space provided.

1. In the _____ of the film, the forces of good overcome the forces of evil in a spectacular battle, full of the most amazing special effects.

2. I was awakened from my reverie when the _____ of freshly brewed coffee suddenly wafted into the room.

3. Though modern science understands the workings of much of the world we live in, certain natural _____ have so far defied explanation.

4. Many contemporary observers regarded Napoleon's self-coronation as Emperor of the French as a clear indication of his overweening _____.

5. Charlie Chaplin's famous characterization of a tramp is a truly masterful blend of humor and _____.

6. Sigmund Freud was one of the first modern scientists to attempt to delve into the mysteries of the human _____.

7. According to the Greek philosopher Aristotle, tragedy aimed at producing a kind of spiritual _____ in the observer, whose soul was cleansed of impurities by experiencing the emotions of pity and terror.

Units 10–12

The Heritage of Literature

Modern English has borrowed a surprising number of words and phrases from the works of famous and not-so-famous writers. One such expression is **quixotic** (page 95), which derives from the name of the main character in the Spanish Renaissance writer Miguel de Cervantes's famous comic novel. A few other expressions of this type are listed below.

bite the hand that feeds you
braggadocio
ragamuffin
salad days

Scrooge
tilt at windmills
yahoo
yeoman service

From the list of expressions above, choose the item that corresponds to each of the brief definitions below. Write the expression in the space provided.

1. empty or pretentious boasting; a braggart _____

> *Source:* the name of a boastful character in Edmund Spenser's epic poem *The Faerie Queene*

2. a miserly and unpleasant person _____

> *Source:* the name of the character in Charles Dickens's *A Christmas Carol* who is noted for his meanness and niggardliness

3. to pursue a course foredoomed to failure _____

> *Source:* a famous episode in *Don Quixote*

4. to show complete ingratitude _____

> *Source:* This expression was first used by the 18th century English orator Edmund Burke in reference to the public's attitude toward government.

5. a crude and brutish person; an unrefined person _____

> *Source:* the name of a race of savage brutes in Jonathan Swift's satire *Gulliver's Travels*

6. one's inexperienced youth _____

> *Source:* a line in Shakespeare's *Antony and Cleopatra* (I, v)

7. a dirty or unkempt child _____

> *Source:* the name of a demon in the medieval epic poem *A Vision of Piers Plowman*, usually ascribed to William Langland

8. effective service, help, or assistance, characterized by hard and steady work _____

> *Source:* Hamlet's tribute to good penmanship in Act V, Scene ii of the play

From the list of expressions above, choose the item that best completes each of the following sentences. Write it in the space provided.

1. He's such a(n) _____ that he won't part with a dime of his money, no matter how worthy the cause.

EYV

2. In my _____ , I was really quite wild, but now that I'm an adult, I lead a very quiet life.

3. My assistant may not be the most creative person under the sun, but she has always done me _____ .

4. His threats were mere _____ that I knew he was much too timid to carry out.

5. Suddenly I was surrounded by a group of grubby little _____, all bellowing at the top of their lungs for a handout.

6. They may think that the policy they are pursuing will result in some useful changes, but I think they are merely _____ .

7. "You have the sensibilities of a(n) _____ and the savoir-faire of a klutz!" I shouted in exasperation.

8. How can you accuse me of _____ simply because I made one or two legitimate criticisms of the company's overtime policy?

Units 13–15

Biblical Expressions

As you may already know, modern English has borrowed a good many words and phrases from the Bible. One such expression is **jeremiad** (page 130), which derives from the name of the Old Testament prophet famous for his eloquent lamentations over the fall of Jerusalem to the Babylonians. A few other expressions drawn from the Bible are listed below.

cast one's bread upon the waters
doubting Thomas
feet of clay
Good Samaritan

hide one's light under a bushel
reap the whirlwind
see the handwriting on the wall
turn the other cheek

From the list of expressions given above, choose the item that corresponds to each of the following brief definitions. Write it in the space provided.

1. to recognize impending disaster   _____

    Source: the incident in which the words "mene, mene, tekel, upharsin" appeared magically on a wall of the palace of Belshazzar, King of Babylon (Daniel 5: 25-31)

2. a questioning or skeptical person; one who habitually has doubts   _____

    Source: an incident involving Christ and one of his disciples (John 20: 25-29)

3. to conceal one's talents; to be excessively modest about one's abilities   _____

    Source: Christ's words to his disciples (Matthew 5: 15)

4. a compassionate person who is ready to help those in distress

_____

> _Source:_ a New Testament parable (Luke 10: 30-37)

5. to bring calamity upon oneself through heedless or foolish actions

_____

> _Source:_ the prophet Hosea's predictions of what would happen to the Israelites because of their impious behavior (Hosea 8: 7)

6. to avoid confrontation or argument   _____

> _Source:_ Christ's instructions to his disciples regarding the proper way to handle hostile people (Matthew 5: 39)

7. to do something that involves a risk or from which profit or gain may not easily be derived

_____

> _Source:_ an expression in Ecclesiastes 9: 1

8. a fatal personal flaw that proves to be one's undoing   _____

> _Source:_ the description of the statue or figure that appeared in Nebuchadnezzar's dream (Daniel 2: 31-34)

> _From the list of expressions given on page 161, choose the item that best completes each of the following sentences. Write it in the space provided._

1. Rather than repay them in kind for their rude and insulting treatment, I decided to _____ and let the matter pass.

2. I'd define a showoff as someone who doesn't _____ .

3. Many a king has pursued foolish policies that were not in his own or his country's best interests and _____ for his efforts.

4. Though I run the risk of being considered an awful _____ , may I repeat my concern about the advisability of the decision you have made?

5. Though the candidate has many fine qualities, his penchant for causing raised eyebrows will, I fear, prove to be his _____ .

6. When the woman was suddenly stricken with a heart attack right in the middle of a crowded street, one or two _____ rushed over to give her what aid they could.

7. "Only the most observant of us actually _____ at that early stage of the race," the Senator confessed.

8. The day he announced his candidacy for President of the United States, he said: "I've _____ ; now I can only hope that some of it comes back sandwiches!"

Working with Parts of Speech

Units 1–3

Verbs

Verbs denote actions or states of being—for example, *strike* and *become*. In Units 1–3 we encountered several useful verbs, including *caterwaul, obfuscate,* and *cozen.* Here are a few more to add to your active vocabulary.

addle	**construe**	**foreclose**	**limn**	**spew**
cogitate	**festoon**	**impale**	**occlude**	

From the list of words above, choose the item that corresponds to each of the brief definitions below. Write the word in the space at the right of the definition and then in the illustrative phrase below it.

1. to pierce with something sharp; to kill by fixing on a sharp stake; to put in a hopeless or inescapable position _____

reenters with Macbeth's head _____ on his sword

2. to shape into decorative strips or bands hanging between two points; generally, to decorate or adorn; to hang down like a pendant _____

since icicles _____ the eaves

3. to close up or block off, obstruct; to bar passage of, shut out; to take in and retain in the interior; *(of the teeth)* to come into proper contact with the opposite teeth in the mouth; *(of weather)* to cut off from the surface of the earth and force aloft _____

_____ the coronary artery

4. to think or think about intently, ponder; to plot, plan _____

carefully _____ his answer

5. to come forth in a flood or gush; to send forth with violence or vigor or in great quantity, vomit; to ooze out, exude _____

continues to _____ molten lava

6. to throw into confusion, confound; to become rotten, spoil; to become confused _____

unused eggs that _____ after several months

7. to draw or paint on a surface; to outline in clear and sharp detail, delineate; to describe _____

never _____ by a master's brush before

8. to shut out, debar, preclude; to bring to an end; to deal with or complete early; to bar or extinguish the right to redeem a mortgage; to hold exclusively _____

_____ on the family farm

9. *(grammar)* to analyze the function and arrangement of words in a sentence; to understand or explain the sense or intention of something in a particular way _____

chose to _____ their actions as treasonable

From the list of words on page 163, choose the item that best completes each of the following sentences. Write the word in the space provided.

1. "Some international problems," the diplomat confessed, "are so recalcitrant as to

_____ the brain and depress the spirits."

2. Freedom of the press, for those who _____ the phrase literally, is the right to publish anything at all, no matter how controversial, offensive, or inflammatory it may be.

3. "I felt," she said, "that if I moved back in with my parents at this juncture in my life, I

would _____ any opportunity, at least in the foreseeable future, for achieving independence and self-sufficiency."

4. Slowly and painfully the old San Franciscan trolley trundled up Telegraph Hill with

dozens of tourists _____ its exterior like so many human garlands on an errant Mardi Gras float.

5. The hulks of sunken ships and other underwater debris so _____ the harbor that the port was virtually useless long after the war had ended.

6. Once he had _____ the enemy ship in the sights of his periscope, the captain of the submarine gave the order to launch the torpedoes.

7. I've always wondered exactly what *The Thinker,* the French sculptor Auguste Rodin's

great statue, is _____ on.

8. For hours on end the strange old man harangued passersby from the vantage of his

soapbox like some Old Testament prophet _____ forth God's wrath at a peccant Israel.

9. There I was, _____ on the horns of a dilemma, not knowing which way to turn; and in my indecision, I all but lost my will to act.

Units 4–6

Nouns

A *noun* names a person, place, thing, quality, action, or idea. For example, *soldier, kitchen, fork, hope, murder,* and *evolution* are all nouns. In Units 4–6 we encountered a number of useful nouns, including *obloquy, genre,* and *prescience.* Here are a few more to add to your active vocabulary.

apocalypse	**exegesis**	**métier**	**preponderance**	**tutelage**
dossier	**hegemony**	**parvenu**	**tocsin**	

From the list of words above, choose the item that corresponds to each of the brief definitions below. Write the word in the space at the right of the definition and then in the illustrative phrase below it.

1. a person who has recently or suddenly risen to an unaccustomed position of wealth or power and is somewhat clumsy or gauche in handling his/her new situation, upstart, nouveau riche, arriviste

_____

a lack of social polish that marked him as a(n) _____

2. an explanation, exposition, or critical interpretation of a text, especially the Bible

_____

a somewhat controversial _____ of Genesis

3. a job, occupation, business, profession, vocation, or trade; an activity in which one excels, forte; a special line of activity; *(collective)* the special techniques that characterize a profession, method

      the _____ of the novelist

4. *(capital A)* a writing that claims to reveal the future, especially the book of Revelation in the New Testament or any of the Judaeo-Christian writings concerning a cosmic cataclysm in which the powers of evil are destroyed; *(lowercase a)* something viewed as a prophetic revelation, prophetic disclosure; in general, any cosmic or general cataclysm

      the Four Horsemen of the _____

5. a guardianship or protectorate; dominion over a foreign country, trusteeship; the state of being under a guardian or protector, dependence; in general, a guiding influence

      rose to stardom under the _____ of George Balanchine

6. a file containing documents and other detailed information about a particular person or subject; any accumulation of documents and reports on a single subject

      kept detailed _____ on his patients

7. an alarm bell; the ringing of an alarm bell; any kind of warning signal; something perceived to resemble an alarm bell

      panicky warnings sounding from the _____'s throat

8. overwhelming influence or authority over someone or something, domination; a state or government possessing such authority

      45 years of Soviet _____ in Eastern Europe

9. a massive superiority in weight, strength, power, or importance; a superiority in number or quantity, vast majority

      the _____ of the evidence

From the list of words on page 164, choose the item that best completes each of the following sentences. Write the word in the space provided.

1. In sharp contrast to Sir Wyvern Moldwarp and his brother, Hippogriff, whose gentle blood is of unimpeachable antiquity, Gillie Gowpen, Esq., the new occupant of

Gaberlunzie Grange, is essentially a(n) _____ whose social prominence in our fair town of Bouking-on-the-Wash is of decidedly contemporary vintage.

2. Eighteenth-century voting regulations were consciously designed to give a numerical

_____ of representatives in the House of Commons to the landed gentry, whose firm support for the revolutionary settlement of 1689 had written "Paid" to Stuart attempts at absolute monarchy.

3. Jefferson once likened the Missouri Compromise of 1820, which essentially divided

the nation into slave states and free, to a(n) _____ that awakened him in the night and filled him with terror.

4. Exploration, rather than warfare, was the essential _____ of the British Navy during those long years of peace.

5. As soon as World War II was over, and the full extent of the horror of Hitler's "final solution" was known, various organizations, on both sides of the Iron Curtain, began to compile extensive _____ on Nazi war criminals, many of whom were eventually hunted down, prosecuted, and convicted.

6. In most ancient societies marriage was looked upon as a sort of rite of passage in which a woman formally exchanged the _____ of her father for that of her husband.

7. "I think you'll concede," Lady Sophonisba Moldwarp observed, "that the somewhat obscure personal symbolism of a poet like T.S. Eliot requires considerably more _____ than the more immediate verses of a rhymester like Sir Arthur Sullivan." "Soitenly," Hippogriff replied.

8. For more than three hundred years after the death of Alexander the Great in 323 B.C., Hellenism exercised an overwhelming cultural _____ on the lands of the Near East.

9. "Who would ever have thought," I asked myself, "that so many would perish in the fiery _____ that rang the curtain down on the tragedy at Waco?"

Units 7–9

Adjectives

An *adjective* describes or qualifies a noun. Among the adjectives we encountered in Units 7–9 were *inchoate, cantankerous,* and *ecumenical.* Here are a few more useful adjectives to add to your active vocabulary.

autochthonous	**demented**	**nugatory**	**puerile**	**swarthy**
condign	**eristic**	**pristine**	**seamy**	

From the list of words above, choose the item that corresponds to each of the brief definitions below. Write the word in the space at the right of the definition and then in the illustrative phrase below it.

1. relating to boyhood, boyish; characteristic of children in general, immature, juvenile; childish, silly   _____

_____ pranks

2. of unsound mind, mad, insane, deranged; marked or caused by insanity   _____

_____ laughter

3. of little or no importance, inconsequential, trifling; having no force, inoperative, invalid   _____

rendered such laws _____

4. forming or resembling a seam; marked with seams, wrinkled; unpleasant; unpresentable; sordid or degraded   _____

the old salt's _____ and weather-beaten visage

5. marked by disputations and hairsplitting or fallacious reasoning; wrangling or otherwise inclined to argue about minutiae _____

_____ by temperament rather than design

6. formed or originating in the place where found; indigenous to a region; endemic, not imported; native, aboriginal _____

_____ viruses like Ebola

7. dark in color, complexion, or cast, dusky _____

"Like some full-breasted swan that takes the flood

. . . with _____ webs" (Tennyson, "Morte d'Arthur")

8. entirely in accord with what is deserved or merited, neither exceeding nor falling short of what one wants; worthy, fitting, or appropriate _____

_____ punishment

9. belonging to the earliest period or state, original, primitive; not spoiled, corrupted, or polluted by the world or civilization, pure; fresh, clean, and new _____

"in all their _____ magnificence and beauty" (Prescott, *The Conquest of Mexico*)

From the list of words on page 166, choose the item that best completes each of the following sentences. Write the word in the space provided.

1. Given the host's decidedly _____ style of interviewing, it is not surprising that the show often descends to the level of mere verbal fisticuffs and captious one-upsmanship.

2. Because the great majority of the volumes in his vast private library remained in the

_____ condition in which they had been received from the bookseller, one could easily tell that Sir Wyvern had little use for reading.

3. In 1810 George III, who had suffered intermittent periods of lunacy since 1780, was

declared hopelessly _____ , and his position as head of state was conferred on his eldest son, the Prince of Wales.

4. The novels of the English writer George Gissing often dealt with somewhat grim or

_____ aspects of London life that "more respectable" novelists shunned on the assumption that one does not air one's dirty linen in public.

5. From one perspective U.S. history until quite late in the nineteenth century can be viewed as the relentless struggle of immigrants from the Old World to displace the

_____ peoples and societies of the North American continent from their immemorial homelands.

6. Personal scandal so discredited Charles Stewart Parnell, the so-called uncrowned king of Ireland, as to render his formerly immense political influence on those who

could actually effect Irish home rule absolutely _____ .

7. One of the main characters in the novel is a strapping young fellow named Evan Dhu —that is, Evan "the Black"—probably so-called because he was of a decidedly

more _____ cast than was customary among Highland Gaels.

8. Despite his great reputation as a profound thinker, I found his remarks at the graduation ceremonies somewhat _____ , perfunctory, and self-evident.

9. Though short of stature, Catherine the Great was "every inch a queen"—truly, as more than one contemporary noted, a most _____ figure to wear the imperial crown of all the Russias.

Units 10–12

Verbs

Verbs can be divided into those that take an object *(transitive verbs)* and those that do not *(intransitive verbs)*. Among the verbs we encountered in Units 10–12 were *adjudicate,* a transitive verb, and *impinge,* an intransitive verb. Here are a few more useful verbs to add to your active vocabulary.

adduce	contravene	glower	molder	succor
chortle	descry	macerate	parse	

From the list of words above, choose the item that corresponds to each of the brief definitions below. Write the word in the space at the right of the definition and then in the illustrative phrase below it.

1. *(trans.)* to cause to waste away by excessive fasting; to cause to become soft or separated into its fundamental parts by immersing in a liquid, steep, soak; *(intrans.)* to soften or wear away _____

_____ fruit in a simple syrup

2. *(trans.)* to break a sentence into its component parts and describe each grammatically; to examine minutely, analyze critically; *(intrans.)* to admit of such an analysis _____

spent hours _____ing and diagramming sentences

3. *(trans.)* to offer as proof, reason, or example in a discussion or argument, cite, present _____

the precedents that I have _____

4. to act or go contrary to, violate; to oppose in an argument, contradict, deny _____

_____ the law

5. *(trans.)* to go to the aid of, help; to provide with supplies, reinforcement, or the like, relieve; to alleviate, mitigate _____

"and _____ the afflicted" (*The Book of Common Prayer,* 1662)

6. *(intrans.)* to sing or chant joyfully; to laugh or chuckle with contemptuous satisfaction or delight; *(trans.)* to express laughingly _____

" 'And hast thou slain the Jabberwock?
Come to my arms, my beamish boy!
O frabjous day! Callooh! Callay!'

He _____ in his joy."
(Lewis Carroll, *Through the Looking-Glass*)

WPS

---

7. *(intrans.)* to stare or look at with smoldering or brooding anger or annoyance, scowl, lower _____

replied by _____ing back at me in silence

8. *(intrans.)* to crumble away into tiny bits, disintegrate, decay; to deteriorate for lack of exercise; *(trans.)* to cause to disintegrate; to fritter away, waste _____

"John Brown's body lies a-_____ing in the grave,
His soul is marching on!"
(Thomas Bishop, "John Brown's Body")

9. *(trans.)* to catch sight of from afar through watchful attention, see, espy; to discover, find out _____

_____ them on the beach far below

From the list of words on page 168, choose the item that best completes each of the following sentences. Write the word in the space provided.

1. "I may not be the most percipient person in the room," the lawyer demurred modestly, "but the evidence I have presented appears on the face of it utterly to

_____ the theory advanced by my opponents."

2. "When I first looked at the broken inscription," the archaeologist admitted, "I was

certain it would not _____ ; but after puzzling over it for some time, I began to see how most of the elements fit together."

3. "In the administration's view, the present situation in Bosnia-Hercegovina is unique," the spokesperson replied, "and for that reason we do not find the historical parallels

_____ by many diplomats at all convincing."

4. We were not so far from the center of the battle that we could not _____ in graphic detail the desperate hand-to-hand struggle in which the combatants were engaged.

5. Unfortunately, the relief column sent to _____ General Gordon and those trapped in Khartoum arrived much too late to raise the siege and effect the proposed rescue.

6. The long period of solitary confinement endured by the prisoner served but to drain

his physical resources and _____ his mental faculties.

7. I could not help _____ just a little over our archenemy the Gaberlunzie Gillies' resounding defeat at the hands of our stalwart home team, the Wyvern Wights, forty-five to zip!

8. "Is it any wonder that your nephew has proved such an incorrigible rake," Lady

Sophonisba rejoined, "when he has spent his entire youth _____ in the fleshpots of the capital?"

9. The altercation finally ended when bystanders separated the two participants, who all

the while _____ silent defiance at each other.

10. The wealth of recordings that Toscanini has left us makes it extremely easy for us to

_____ the reasons for his overwhelming dominance of the musical circles of his time.

Units 13–15

Nouns

As you know, nouns are subdivided into *common nouns,* naming something general (for example, *country*), and *proper nouns,* naming something particular (for example, *United States of America*). The nouns presented in VOCABULARY WORKSHOP are almost exclusively common nouns. Among those we encountered in Units 13–15 is *jeremiad.* This word is a common noun derived from a proper noun, the name of the Old Testament prophet Jeremiah. Here are a few more useful common nouns to add to your active vocabulary.

aggregate	**denouement**	**nexus**	**provenance**	**scion**
circumlocution	**factotum**	**panoply**	**regimen**	

From the list of words above, choose the item that corresponds to each of the brief definitions below. Write the word in the space at the right of the definition and then in the illustrated phrase below it.

1. a suit of armor; ceremonial dress; any protective covering; an impressive or gorgeous array; a display of all characteristic traits or accessories; pieces of armor arranged as an emblem, symbol, or trophy _____

"He heard the groaning of the oak,
And donn'd at once his sable cloak,
As warrior, at the battle-cry

Invests him with his _____ ."
(Scott, *Waverley*)

2. a small part of one plant used for grafting onto another, larger plant; a child, offspring, or descendant _____

experiments involving _____ and rootstocks

3. all the parts of something loosely considered as a whole; all the elements or individuals in a particular group or category, sum total; any of several hard materials used for making concrete when mixed with cement _____

amounted in the _____ to 600 million dollars

4. a systematic plan, especially one to improve a patient's health; a regular course of action; government, rule _____

the strenuous daily physical _____ of a top athlete

5. a connection or link; a connected group or series; the focus or center of something _____

the _____ of cause and effect

6. the use of an unnecessarily large number of words or roundabout expressions to convey an idea, periphrasis; any linguistic evasion _____

a studiously diplomatic _____

7. the final outcome of the plot in a drama or other literary work; the outcome of any long or complex sequence of events _____

the unexpectedly grisly _____ of the novel

8. a person having many different responsibilities or involved in many different activities, jack-of-all-trades, girl or guy Friday   _____

    her secretary and general _____

9. the source or origin of something, especially something rare or valuable; a detailed history of the ownership of a work of art or the like   _____

    the date and _____ of the tapestries

From the list of words on page 170, choose the item that best completes each of the following sentences. Write the word in the space provided.

1. In Dickens's day, the High Court of Chancery was just one of a(n) _____ of interlocking judicial institutions of immemorial antiquity—that is, just one small cog in the mighty machine of the law.

2. "One can only guess at the _____ of these rumors," she asserted, "but wherever they came from, they should be discounted out of hand."

3. One recent historian has characterized the 70-odd-year dialog between the government of the Soviet Union and its citizens as a vast web of half-truths,

    _____ , and double-talk.

4. The book recounts in vivid detail the tortured relations between the early Stuart kings

and Parliament from their inception in 1603 until their bloody _____ on the scaffold outside the Banqueting Room at Whitehall in 1649.

5. During the dark days of the French Revolution the views expressed in a short pamphlet entitled "Driving a Tumbril for Fun and Profit" by one of Gillie's forebears, a carter by trade, so offended the sensibilities of an ancestor of Sir Wyvern that the latter ceased to speak to or deal with the former, and this social and economic coldness hardened into a tradition that has been steadfastly maintained by all

subsequent _____ of the respective families down to the present.

6. In like manner, Seamus MacWeeble, Sir Wyvern's butler, valet, amanuensis, and

general _____ , also felt it incumbent, as *majordomo* and *tenens in capite* (chief supporter) of an ancient and much revered knightly lineage, to forbid his family all intercourse or communication with the offending carter's descendants, going even so far as to spurn sitting in the same meeting-house pew as any representative of the proscribed brood.

7. On days of high festival it was Sir Wyvern's immemorial custom to dine with his counterpart from the north, the aged chieftain of a most ancient Scottish clan, who invariably appeared at these solemn ceremonies with, as the saying goes, "his tail

on"—that is, with a full _____ of supporters, vassals, and dependents, including his bodyguard and his own personal bard.

8. The _____ of total proscription to which Sir Wyvern and MacWeeble, as the mentors of a well-regulated society, subjected the offending brood of Gowpen in no way affected Gillie's ability to reproduce both children and money, so that he and his wife, Howdie, slowly but ineluctably rose in social standing in the neighborhood despite the efforts of the social engineers at Moldwarp-Honor.

9. Needless to say, the Gowpens' rise to prominence did not sit well at Moldwarp-Honor, but Sir Wyvern consoled himself with the thought that, however impressive,

the _____ of goods and kin that Gillie had amassed in no way held a candle to the simple but inestimable blessing of being "to the manor born."

Index

The following tabulation lists all the basic words taught in the various units of this workbook, as well as those introduced in the *Vocabulary of Vocabulary, Building with Word Roots, Enhancing Your Vocabulary,* and *Working with Parts of Speech* sections. The number after each item indicates the page on which the word is introduced, but it may also appear in exercises on later pages.